Compiler Design

Reinhard Wilhelm · Helmut Seidl

Compiler Design

Virtual Machines

 Springer

Prof. Dr. Reinhard Wilhelm
Universität des Saarlandes
FB Informatik
Postfach 15 11 50
66041 Saarbrücken Saarland
Germany
wilhelm@cs.uni-sb.de

Prof. Dr. Helmut Seidl
TU München
Fak. Informatik
Boltzmannstr. 3
85748 Garching
Germany
seidl@in.tum.de

ISBN 978-3-642-14908-5   e-ISBN 978-3-642-14909-2
DOI 10.1007/978-3-642-14909-2
Springer Heidelberg Dordrecht London New York

ACM Codes: D.1, D.3, D.2

Cover design: KuenkelLopka GmbH

Printed on acid-free paper

Springer is part of Springer Science+Business Media (www.springer.com)

For Margret, Hannah, Eva, Barbara

R.W.

For Kerstin and Anna

H.S.

Preface

Compilers for high-level programming languages are software systems which are both large and complex. Nonetheless, they have particular characteristics that differentiate them from the majority of other software systems.

Their functionality is (almost) completely well-defined. Ideally, there exist completely formal, or at least rather precise, specifications of the source and target languages. Often additional specifications of the interfaces to the operating system, to programming environments, and to other compilers and libraries are available.

The compilation task can be naturally divided into subtasks. This subdivision results in a modular structure, which, by the way, also leads to a canonical structure of the common compiler design books.

Already in the Fifties it was recognized that the implementation of application systems directly in machine language is both difficult and error-prone, leading to programs that become obsolete as quickly as the computers they were developed for. With the development of higher level machine independent programming languages came the need to offer compilers that are able to translate programs of such programming languages into machine language.

Given this basic challenge, the different subtasks of compilation have been the subject of intensive research since the Fifties. For the subtask of syntactic analysis of programs, concepts from formal language and automata theory, such as regular languages, finite automata, context-free grammars, and pushdown automata were borrowed and were further developed in view of the particular use. The theoretical foundation of the problem was so well-developed that the realization of the components required for syntax analysis could be (almost) completely automated: instead of being implemented *by hand* these components are mainly generated from specifications, in this case context-free grammars. Such automatic generation is also the aim for other components of compilers, although is has not always been achieved yet.

This book is not intended to be a cookbook for compilers. Thus, one will not find recipes like: "To build a compiler of source language X into machine language Y, take ... ". Our presentation instead reflects the special characteristics of compiler design, specially the existence of precise specifications of the subtasks. We invest some effort to understand these precisely and to provide adequate concepts for their systematic treatment. Ideally, those concepts can build the foundation of a process of automatic generation.

This book is intended for students of Informatics. Knowledge of at least one imperative programming language is assumed. For the chapters on the translation of functional and logic programming languages it is certainly helpful to know a modern functional language and the basic concepts of the logic language PROLOG. On the other hand, these chapters can help to achieve a more profound understanding of such programming languages.

Structure of This Book

For the new edition of the book Wilhelm/Maurer: *Compiler Design*, we decided to divide the contents in multiple volumes. This first volume describes *what* a compiler does: thus, what correspondence it establishes between a source and a target program. To achieve this, for each of an imperative, functional, logic, and object-oriented programming language, a suitable *virtual* machine (called *abstract* machine in previous editions) is specified, and the compilation of programs of each source language into the language of the corresponding virtual machine is presented in detail.

The virtual machines of the previous edition have been fully revised and modernized with the aim of simplifying the translation schemes and, if necessary, to complete them. Compared to before, the various chosen architectures and instruction sets have been made more uniform to clearly highlight the similarities, as well as the differences, of the language concepts. Perhaps the most obvious, if not the most important, feature that readers of earlier editions will easily recognize is that the stack of virtual machines are growing upwards and no longer from *top to bottom*.

Fragments of real programming languages have been used in all example programming languages. As the imperative source language, the programming language PASCAL has been replaced with C – a choice for a more realistic approach. A subset of C++ serves again as object-oriented language. Compared to the presentation of the second edition, however, a detailed discussion of multiple inheritance has been omitted.

In this book, the starting point of the translations of imperative, functional, logic, and object-oriented programs is always a structured internal representation of the source program, for which already simple additional information, such as scope of variables or type information has been added. Later we will call such an analyzed source program an *annotated abstract syntax* of the program.

In the subsequent volumes, the *how* of the compilation process will be described. There, we deal with the question of how to divide the compilation process into a sequence of phases: which tasks each individual phase has to cover, which techniques are used in them, how to describe formally what they do, and how, perhaps, a compiler module can be automatically created out of such a specification.

Acknowledgments

Besides the coworkers of previous editions, we would like to thank all the students who participated in courses again and again using different versions of virtual machines and who gave us invaluable feedback. The visualization of the virtual machines by Peter Ziewer added a lot to the comprehension. For subtle insight into the semantics of C++ and Java we thank Thomas Gawlitza and Michael Petter. Special thanks go to Jörg Herter, who inspected multiple versions of the book carefully for inconsistencies and who drew our attention to multiple mistakes and oddities.

In the meantime we wish the eager reader lots of fun with this volume and hope that the book will whet her appetite to quickly create her own compiler for the favorite programming language.

Saarbrücken and München, May 2010   Reinhard Wilhelm, Helmut Seidl

Further material for this book can be found on the following Web page:

http://www2.informatik.tu-muenchen.de/~seidl/compilers/

Contents

1

Introduction

1.1 High-Level Programming Languages

Today programs are mainly written in problem-oriented, high-level programming languages. These programming languages abstract (up to various degree) from the structure and the details of the hardware on which the programs are supposed to be executed. The four most important classes of universal programming languages are:

- *Imperative languages*, such as ALGOL60, ALGOL68, FORTRAN, COBOL, PASCAL, ADA, MODULA-2, or C closely follow the structure of the von Neumann architecture which forms the basis of almost all commercially available computers. This architecture consists of an (active) central processing unit (CPU), a (passive) memory, and a bus for data transfer between central processing unit and memory.
- *Functional languages*, such as LISP, SML, OCAML, and HASKELL do not provide explicit statements for directing the control flow. The central concepts are expressions which are to be evaluated, variables denoting values (not memory locations). Also functions are considered as values which may appear both as arguments to functions and be returned as results.
- *Logic programming languages* such as PROLOG and its various dialects are based on an operational view of first-order predicate logic. The execution mechanism is *resolution*, a process that was developed for proving implications.
- *Object-oriented programming languages* such as SMALLTALK, C++ and JAVA are mostly imperative. They support data abstraction and an *evolutionary* style of software development.

Besides these classes, various special-purpose languages exist such as:

- Hardware description languages, such as VHDL. These are used for the specification of computers and computer components. Such specifications can describe the functional behavior, the hierarchical composition, and the geometrical placement of components.

R. Wilhelm, H. Seidl, *Compiler Design*, DOI 10.1007/978-3-642-14909-2_1,

- Command languages of operating systems. As primitive constructs, these offer the invocation of system functions and user programs and to orchestrate multiple of these programs and system functions to cooperate in a coordinated way, the creation and termination of processes, and the discovery and handling of exceptions.
- Specification languages for printed pages, graphical objects, or animations. One example is the programming language POSTSCRIPT from Adobe, which specifies the graphical appearance of each page for the printer. For the specification of animations, not only the geometric dimensions of the objects to be presented must be described, but also the chronological ordering and possibly planned reactions to events.
- Languages for the processing of structured documents. In recent years XML has succeeded as a standard format for representing structured data. The range of applications and the extent of circulation in the Internet led to numerous further standards, from XSCHEMA for the detailed description of document types, to the XML transformation language XSLT and the XML query language XQUERY, all the way to formalisms related to Web services or business processes.

1.2 Implementation of Programming Languages

In order to run programs of a certain programming language L on a given hardware, this programming language has to be made available, that is, *implemented*, on this hardware. This is possible in various ways. Implementations can be divided into interpretation- and translation-based approaches.

1.2.1 Interpreters

Consider a programming language L. An interpreter I_L takes as input a program p_L written in L together with input data e for p_L and generates output data a. Since the interpretation of p_L may result in an error, I_L has the functionality

$$I_L : L \times D \rightarrow D \times \{error\},$$

where, for simplicity, both input and output data are taken from the same set D. The execution of the program p_L with input data e and output data a can therefore be described by the equation

$$I_L(p_L, e) = a$$

Characteristic for an interpreter is that it works on the program p_L and the input e simultaneously. Every construct c of the program is analyzed and interpreted as it is encountered during the execution – even if c has already been encountered. No information about the program is exploited which could be extracted by inspection of the program as a whole, such as the set of declared variables in a block, a function, or a block, although such information could allow for a more efficient management of the program variables.

1.2.2 Compilers

The goal of compilation is to avoid the inefficiencies incurred by plain interpretation. Compilation relies upon *precomputation* which sometimes takes the form of *partial evaluation* or *mixed computation*.

Unlike an interpreter I_L, which receives and processes both the program p_L and the input data e at the same time, processing of the program and processing the input data is now assigned to two distinct phases. First, the program p_L is *preprocessed* independent of the input data, that is, analyzed and converted into a form that allows the program to be executed efficiently on arbitrary input data later. The hope is that the additional effort of preprocessing the program is amortized by the gain in efficiency of the residual program when executed once or multiple times on the input data.

Preprocessing of programs typically consists of translating the program p_L, which is written in the language L, from now on called *source language*, into the machine, or assembly, language M of the real or virtual processor architecture. The phase at which this translation occurs is called *compile-time*. The resulting program p_M is called the *target program* of p_L.

By translating source programs into target programs, the two sources of inefficiencies of interpretation are removed. Each program is analyzed once at compile-time; the resulting target program, assuming it is a program in the machine language of a real computer, requires no further analysis but decoding of the instruction opcodes by the computer's central processing unit. Efficient access to the values of variables is possible via a memory management scheme that assigns locations with fixed (relative) addresses to all variables in the program. These addresses are directly embodied into the generated target program.

The resulting target program p_M is later executed on the input data e. This phase, which follows the compile-time, is called *run-time*. We expect that the target program p_M, produced by compilation, produces exactly the same output for input e that the interpreter produces when interpreting the source program p_L together with e. If we consider the machine M as an interpreter I_M for its own machine language, then the minimum requirement for compilation, thus, can be formalized by:

$$I_L(p_L, e) = a \quad \Longrightarrow \quad I_M(p_M, e) = a$$

for all legal programs p_L of the source language L and all legal inputs e for p_L. Beyond this, various error situations may occur. On the one hand, p_L may contain syntax errors or violations of context conditions given in the specification of the language L and, thus, strictly speaking, would not belong to L. Then p_L should be rejected by the compiler. If these errors refer to parts of the program that the interpreter never touches during execution with e, interpretation may still run successfully. On the other hand, the interpreter I_L, even though p_L is syntactically correct and satisfies the context conditions, may detect a (run-time) error during execution with input e. If I_L is considered as the definition of the semantics of L, then the execution of the generated target program p_M on e must also run into this error – even if a static analysis has found out that the subcomputation within which the error occurs does not contribute to producing the outputs of the program p_L.

1.2.3 Real and Virtual Machines

Programmers typically think of *real* computers to execute their programs. Real computers are commercially available in large quantities as real hardware, that is, boards equipped with some processor, memory chips, and anything else that is needed. In this case, the target language of compilation is given by the processor architecture.

Still, when generating code for a high-level programming language, one quickly realizes that it would be convenient if dedicated instructions could be used for compilation, which are not available in the given instruction set of the processor. Also, the instruction sets of modern processors change too often to tailor a compiler exactly for one specific hardware architecture. Such a design could mean that the compiler for the next generation of processors a few years later would have to be written from scratch.

Already during the implementation of early ALGOL60 compilers the idea came up, to generate code for a simple, idealized *virtual* machine first, whose instructions then only had to be implemented for the various concrete target processors. This approach became very popular with the advent of PASCAL, whose implementation was distributed over the whole world by means of a carefully designed virtual machine and compiler for that machine. The compilation of modern programming languages, such as PROLOG, HASKELL, or JAVA are all based on this principle. This approach enhances the portability of the compiler. It also simplifies the compilation itself, because now an instruction set can be designed that is well suited to the programming language to be compiled.

New applications in the area of the Internet have made, for some time now, the idea of virtual machines even more attractive. The portability gained through a virtual machine can be used to realize *platform-independent* systems, that is, systems which run under different operating systems. Taking this idea a little further, code can be made *mobile* and be distributed via the Internet. This is, among others, the idea of the programming language JAVA.

Executing foreign code on one's own computer has not only advantages but also incurs the danger of malicious attacks. Virtual machines offer a solution for this scenario: as the code is not executed directly by the hardware, the behavior of the code to be executed can be monitored and its access rights to the resources of the computer can be restricted. This has also been called *sandboxing*.

In this book we present virtual machines for imperative, functional, logic, and object-oriented programming languages. Of particular interest are the *translation schemes*, which explain how sequences of virtual machine instructions are generated for the concrete language constructs of a programming language.

1.2.4 Combined Compilation and Interpretation

Various combinations of compilation and interpretation are possible. Often when source programs are compiled into the machine language of a virtual machine, the virtual intructions are interpreted by an interpreter. The language of the virtual machine can, however, be further compiled, into the language of a real processor. The latter is also called *native code*. The second compilation may take place at run-time, in which case it is called *Just-In-Time compilation (JIT)*. The two phases, compile-time and run-time are thus combined. The JIT compiler is invoked at run-time, typically for fragments of code only, e.g., for a function or a particular loop, often at the exact time when the given fragment is to be executed or repeatedly executed.

The aim of JIT compilation is to combine efficiency with portability. The first compilation step, which is usually complex, is only done once. The second step, the compilation of the intermediate code, is much simpler. The generated native code is (hopefully) efficient. Often, efficiency is further enhanced by optimizations such as constant propagation or inlining of functions. The generated code is stored in a cache memory, such that program fragments need not be compiled repeatedly.

The first and second compilation also need not necessarily occur on the same computer. The first step may, for example, take place on the computer of the programmer. There, a portable intermediate code is generated in the language of a virtual machine. This code may be downloaded onto a different computer where the second compilation creates (preferably efficient) native code for this computer.

1.3 General References

An overview of the history of programming languages and programming language concepts can be found in, among others, [Seb05, Sco05, TN06]. The semantics of the hardware description language VHDL is described in [Ped04]. The page description language POSTSCRIPT can be found in [Inc99]. An overview of ACTIONSCRIPT for the execution of flash animations can be found in [Hau06]. The XML transformation language XSLT-2.0 is explained in detail in [Kay04]. For the XML query language XQUERY we refer to [KCD$^+$03, Bru04]. An introduction to the work of W3C standards on Web services and business processes is presented in [ACKM03]. Various uses of virtual machines, in particular in the area of operating systems, are described in [SN05].

2

Imperative Programming Languages

We start our presentation with the translation of an imperative programming language. As an example, we consider a subset of the programming language C. Our target language for translation is the instruction set of a suitable virtual machine, which has been specificly designed for this purpose. This virtual machine is called *C-Machine* or CMA for short.

2.1 Language Concepts and Their Compilation

Imperative programming languages offer, among other things, the following concepts, which have to be mapped onto concepts, and control sequences of virtual or real computers:

Variables.   Variables are containers for data objects whose contents (value) can be changed during the execution of the program. Values may change through the execution of *statements* such as assignments. Multiple variables can be grouped into aggregates such as arrays and records (structs). The current values of the variables at any given time constitute parts of the *state* of the program execution at this particular time. Variables in programs are identified by individual *names*. As constants, functions, etc., are also identified by names, these names are called *variable identifiers*, *constant identifiers*, etc., if these kinds of names are to be differentiated. Variable identifiers must be mapped to memory locations, which during program execution will contain their values. If the programming language provides functions with local variables, new *instances* of the local variable identifier are created at function calls. This means that also new memory locations must be allocated to these. When the function terminates, the locations for the local instances can again be released. This kind of memory management can conveniently be implemented by means of a run-time stack.

Expressions.   Expressions are terms consisting of constants, names, and operators which can be *evaluated* to values. In general, their values depend on the current program state, since each evaluation of an expression e uses the current values of the variables occurring in e.

R. Wilhelm, H. Seidl, *Compiler Design*, DOI 10.1007/978-3-642-14909-2_2,
© Springer-Verlag Berlin Heidelberg 2010

Explicit Specification of Control Flow.   Most imperative programming languages provide a jump statement, **goto**, which can be translated directly into the unconditional jump instruction of the target machine. Higher-level control constructs such as conditional statements (*if*) or iterative statements (*while, do-while, for*) are compiled by means of *conditional jumps*. A conditional jump typically follows an instruction sequence for the evaluation of a condition. Case distinctions (*switch-case*) can be efficiently realized through *indexed jumps*. Thereby the jump target address, given in the instruction, is modified according to a previously calculated value.

Functions.   Functions and procedures serve as *functional abstraction*, which creates a new statement from a possibly complex statement or sequence of statements. A *call* to this newly defined statement at a program location executes the sequences of statements specified by the definition of the function. After its completion, execution returns with the value computed by the function — given there is any. If the function has *formal parameters*, the function can be called with different *actual parameters*. For the implementation of functions, the instruction set of the machine should provide a jump instruction that memorizes its origin so that control can return to the location of the call. The body of the function must be supplied with the actual parameters at each evaluation (call). These parameters together with the instances of local variables, are conveniently maintained by a stack-style memory management, which is often supported by dedicated machine instructions.

2.2 The Architecture of the C-Machine

Each virtual machine provides a set of *instructions*, which are executed on a virtual hardware. This virtual hardware is mostly *emulated* in software. The execution state is thereby saved in data structures, which are accessed by the instructions and managed by the *run-time system*.

For the sake of clarity, we introduce the architecture and the instructions step by step, as and when required for translating concepts from the source language. We start by introducing the basic memory layout, some registers, and the *main execution cycle* of the C-Machine.

The C-Machine has a *main memory S* of length $maxS + 1$. At its lower end, that is, from address 0 onwards, lies a *stack* that can grow and shrink. The register *SP* (Stack Pointer) always points to the topmost location in the stack. For all instructions of the virtual machine, we adopt the convention that their operands are expected on top of the stack and that their results (if any) are also delivered there. As a simplification, we assume that values of the scalar types fit into one memory location of main memory. As scalar types, we only consider **int** and pointer types, that is, addresses.

The *program store* of the C-Machine contains the program to be executed. It has length $maxC + 1$. At each clock cycle, one instruction of the C-Machine is fetched from some location of the program store for execution. The *Program Counter*, the register *PC*, always contains the address of the next instruction to be executed. This is loaded into an *Instruction Register, IR*, and subsequently executed. Before execution, the content of the program counter *PC* is incremented by 1, which in a sequential

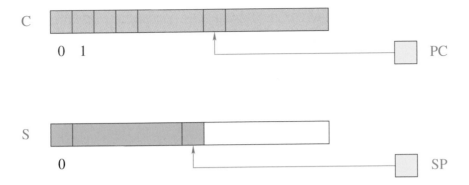

Fig. 2.1. The memory layout of the C-Machine and the registers *PC* and *SP*

execution causes the *PC* to point to the next instruction to be executed. If the current instruction is a jump, it overwrites the contents of the program counter *PC* with its target address.

Thus, the main execution cycle of the C-Machine is given by:

$$\text{while (true)} \{$$
$$IR \leftarrow C[PC]; PC++;$$
$$execute\ (IR);$$
$$\}$$

At the start of program execution, the register *PC* contains the value 0. Program execution, thus, starts with the execution of the instruction in $C[0]$. The C-Machine stops by executing the instruction **halt**. The execution of this instruction exits the execution cycle and returns control back to the operating system. The return value of the program is given by the contents of some dedicated memory location. Since access to the memory location $S[0]$ is forbidden, we assume here that this is the location with the address 1.

2.3 Simple Expressions and Assignments

In this section, we introduce the translation of arithmetic and logic expressions. Each expression must be translated into an instruction sequence whose execution results in the (current) value of the expression. Consider, for example, the expression $(1 + 7) \cdot (2 + 5)$. What does an instruction sequence that evaluates this expression and pushes its result onto the stack look like?

If the expression consists of just one constant, e.g., 7, this task is easy. Only one instruction is needed that pushes a given value onto the stack. For this purpose, we introduce the instruction **loadc** q for any constant q (Fig. 2.2).

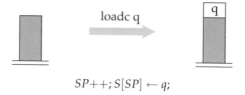

$$SP++; S[SP] \leftarrow q;$$

Fig. 2.2. The instruction **loadc** q

The instruction **loadc** q does not require further arguments. It pushes the value of the constant q onto the stack.

Consider an expression which consists of an operator applied to operands. In order to evaluate such an expression, the operands, here $(1+7)$ and $(2+5)$, are recursively evaluated first, and their values returned on top of the stack. The application of the operator, here $\cdot$, is then evaluated by consuming these intermediate results from the stack and instead pushing the value of the whole expression onto the stack.

We will frequently encounter translation schemes that proceed by recursion on the structure of a program fragment (here: expressions). This recursion is supported by our design decision that arithmetic, logic, and comparison instructions expect their operands on top of the stack and then replace them with their respective results. In Fig. 2.3, the behavior of these instructions is exemplified by the instruction *mul*.

The instruction **mul** expects two arguments on top of the stack, multiplies them,

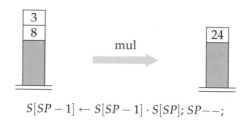

$$S[SP - 1] \leftarrow S[SP - 1] \cdot S[SP]; SP--;$$

Fig. 2.3. The instruction **mul**

thereby consuming them, and then pushes the result onto the stack. The remaining binary arithmetic and logical instructions **add**, **sub**, **div**, **mod**, **and**, **or**, as well as the comparisons **eq**, **neq**, **le**, **leq**, **gr**, and **geq**, work analogously.

Comparison operators also expect two operands at the top of the stack, compare them, and push the result of the comparison onto the stack. The result is supposed to be a logical value, thus representing *true* or *false*. In the case of C, logical values are represented as integer values: 0 denotes *false*, all other values *true*. Figure 2.4 shows how the instruction **leq** compares two integer values.

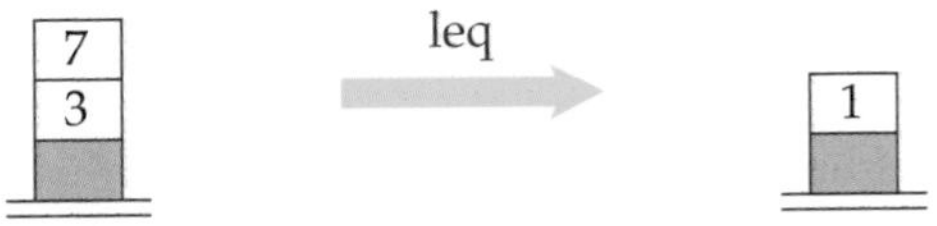

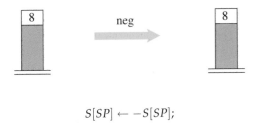

$$S[SP-1] \leftarrow S[SP-1] \leq S[SP];\ SP--;$$

Fig. 2.4. The instruction **leq**

Unary instructions, such as **neg** and **not** consume only one operand. As they also return one value as result, they thus replace the value on top of the stack. As an example we show the instruction **neg** that flips the sign of a number (Fig. 2.5).

$$S[SP] \leftarrow -S[SP];$$

Fig. 2.5. The instruction **neg**

For the expression $1 + 7$, the following instruction sequence is generated:

loadc 1;   **loadc** 7;   **add**

Figure 2.6 shows how this instruction sequence is executed at run-time.

Fig. 2.6. Executing the instruction sequence for $1 + 7$

The instruction sequences to be generated for a statement or an expression are specified by code-functions. These functions receive program fragments as argument. They decompose their argument recursively, assemble instruction sequences for each of the components and combine these to an instruction sequence for the whole program fragment. Here, we are not concerned with analyzing the syntax of C programs, that is, with identifying their syntactical structures. Also, we assume that the input program is *type-correct* and that the *type* of each variable, each function and each subexpression is available.

Program variables are allocated in the main memory S where their values are *stored* in memory locations. The generated code uses the addresses of these locations to load the current values of the variables or to save new values (see Fig. 2.7).

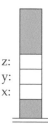

z:
y:
x:

Fig. 2.7. The implementation of variables

Therefore, the code-functions require a function ρ which assigns to each variable x its address in main memory. The function ρ is called *address environment*. As we will see later, the address of a variable is in fact a *relative address*, that is, a constant difference between two absolute addresses in S, namely the address of the location of this variable and the initial address of a memory area, which we will later call a *frame* or *stack frame*. Such a frame will contain space for the instances of all variables, parameters, etc., of a function. For the moment, we may assume that $\rho(x)$ is the address of x relative to the beginning of S.

In imperative languages, variables can be used in two ways. Consider for example the assignment $x \leftarrow y + 1$. For variable y, it is the value that is required to determine the value of the expression $y + 1$. The value of variable x, on the other hand, is not important. For variable x, the address of the memory location is required that holds the value of x. The newly computed value needs to be stored in this memory location. We conclude that, when translating assignments, a variable identifier that occurs on the left side of the assignment has to be compiled differently from a variable identifier that occurs on the right side. From the variable identifier on the left, the address of its memory location is required. This value is called *left value* (L-value) of the identifier. From the variable identifier that occurs on the right, its value is required, more precisely, the contents of the memory cell associated with the identifier. This value is called the *right value* (R-value) of the identifier.Our code functions therefore may be subscripted with L or R. The function code_L generates code for computing the L-value while the function code_R generates code for computing the R-value. The function code (without subscript) translates statements, statement sequences, function definitions or whole programs. We may note already here that, while every expression has an R-value, not every expression has an L-value. A simple example is the expression $y + 1$. The value of this expression only temporarily occurs on top of the stack and therefore may not be accessed via a fixed address.

Figure 2.8 contains the code functions $code_R$ and $code_L$ for some expressions. The L-value of a variable x is provided directly by the address environment. To

$$code_R\ (e_1 + e_2)\ \rho = code_R\ e_1\ \rho$$
$$code_R\ e_2\ \rho$$
add
// analogous for the other binary operators

$$code_R\ (-e)\ \rho\quad = code_R\ e\ \rho$$
neg
// analogous for other unary operators

$$code_R\ q\ \rho\qquad = \textbf{loadc}\ q$$
$$code_L\ x\ \rho\qquad = \textbf{loadc}\ \rho(x)$$
$$code_R\ x\ \rho\qquad = code_L\ x\ \rho$$
load

Fig. 2.8. The definitions of $code_R$ and $code_L$ for some expressions

determine the R-value of x, however, an instruction s required which allows us to replace the address of a memory location on top of the stack with its contents. For this purpose, we introduce the instruction **load** (Fig. 2.9).

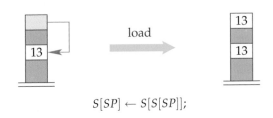

$$S[SP] \leftarrow S[S[SP]];$$

Fig. 2.9. The instruction **load**

In the programming language C, assignments such as $x \leftarrow y + 1$ are *expressions*. The value of this expression is the value of the right side of the assignment. The R-value on the left side of the assignment changes, by means of a *side-effect* when evaluating the assignment expression. For the translation of an assignment, an instruction **store** (Fig. 2.10) is required. The instruction **store** expects two arguments on top of the stack: a value w and, above it, an address a. Then the value w is stored into memory at address a while the value w is returned on top of the stack. In an address environment $\rho = \{x \mapsto 4, y \mapsto 7\}$ the following sequence of instructions computes the R-value of $x \leftarrow y + 1$:

loadc 7; **load**; **loadc** 1; **add**; **loadc** 4; **store**

$$S[S[SP]] \leftarrow S[SP-1]; SP--;$$

Fig. 2.10. The instruction **store**

First the value of the right side is computed. Then follows an instruction sequence for computing the L-value of the left side, in our case **loadc** 4. The assignment itself is eventually carried out by the instruction **store**. In general, an assignment is translated as follows:

$$\text{code}_R \ (x \leftarrow e) \ \rho = \text{code}_R \ e \ \rho$$
$$\text{code}_L \ x \ \rho$$
$$\textbf{store}$$

Example 2.3.1 Consider a program with three *int* variables a, b, c. The address environment ρ maps a, b, c onto the addresses $5, 6$, and 7, respectively. The translation of the assignment $a \leftarrow (b + (b \cdot c))$ proceeds as follows:

$\text{code}_R \ (a \leftarrow (b + (b \cdot c))) \ \rho$
$= \text{code}_R \ (b + (b \cdot c)) \ \rho; \text{code}_L \ a \ \rho; \ \textbf{store}$
$= \text{code}_R \ b \ \rho; \text{code}_R \ (b \cdot c) \ \rho; \textbf{add}; \text{code}_L \ a \ \rho; \ \textbf{store}$
$= \textbf{loadc 6; load;} \ \text{code}_R \ (b \cdot c) \ \rho; \textbf{add}; \ \text{code}_L \ a \ \rho; \textbf{store}$
$= \textbf{loadc 6; load;} \ \text{code}_R \ b \ \rho; \text{code}_R \ c \ \rho; \textbf{mul}; \textbf{add}; \text{code}_L \ a \ \rho; \textbf{store}$
$= \textbf{loadc 6; load; loadc 6; load;} \ \text{code}_R \ c \ \rho; \textbf{mul}; \textbf{add}; \text{code}_L \ a \ \rho; \textbf{store}$
$= \textbf{loadc 6; load; loadc 6; load; loadc 7; load; mul; add; loadc 5; store}$

□

In our examples, certain patterns reappear again and again and always lead to similar instruction sequences. The translation often generates instruction sequences that load the value of a constant address (that is, an address known at compile-time) and then uses this address either to load the contents of this memory location or to store a value there. As an optimization, special instructions could be introduced for these tasks:

$$
\begin{array}{lcl}
\textbf{loada } q & = & \textbf{loadc } q \\
 & & \textbf{load} \\
 & & \\
\textbf{storea } q & = & \textbf{loadc } q \\
 & & \textbf{store}
\end{array}
$$

The new instructions may increase the efficiency of the generated code: on the one hand, the generated code becomes shorter; on the other hand, an implementation of, for example, the instruction **loada** 7 may proceed more efficiently than first creating the constant 7 on the stack, and then overwriting it in the next step with the contents of the memory location with address 7.

2.4 Statements and Statement Sequences

In C, if e is an expression, then $e;$ is a *statement*. Statements do not return values. The value of the Stack Pointer SP must, therefore, be the same before and after the execution of the instruction sequence generated for a statement. Thus, the statement $e;$ is translated as follows:

$$
\text{code } (e;) \, \rho = \text{code}_R \, e \, \rho
$$
$$
\textbf{pop}
$$

where the instruction **pop** removes the top element of the stack (Fig. 2.11).

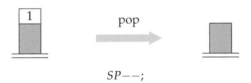

$$
SP--;
$$

Fig. 2.11. The instruction **pop**

If we are able to generate code for one individual statement, it is easy to also generate code for sequences of statements. For that, the code sequences for the individual statements in the sequence are concatenated:

$$
\begin{array}{lll}
\text{code } (s \, ss) \, \rho = & \text{code } s \, \rho \\
& \text{code } ss \, \rho \\
& \quad // \quad s \text{ is a statement, } ss \text{ is a sequence of statements} \\
\text{code } \varepsilon \, \rho \quad = & \quad // \quad \text{an empty sequence of statements}
\end{array}
$$

2.5 Conditional and Iterative Statements

Let us now turn to conditional and iterative statements, usually called loops. In the following, we present schemes for the translation of one-sided and two-sided *if* statements:

$$\textbf{if } (e) \; s$$
$$\textbf{if } (e) \; s_1 \; \textbf{else } s_2$$

as well as for *while* and *for* loops:

$$\textbf{while } (e) \; s$$
$$\textbf{for } (e_1; e_2; e_3) \; s$$

where e, e_i are expressions and s, s_i are single statements or statement sequences that are enclosed in a block.

For deviating from a linear sequence of execution, suitable *jump* instructions are required. *Unconditional* jumps redirect program execution to a fixed given location. *Conditional* jumps perform the jump only if a certain condition is satisfied. In our case, this condition is satisfied if the top element of the stack equals 0 (Fig. 2.12). Instead of absolute instruction addresses as in our definition, *relative* addresses could

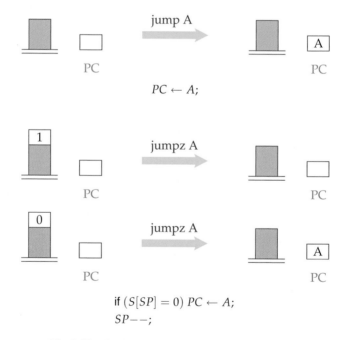

$$PC \leftarrow A;$$

$$\text{if } (S[SP] = 0) \; PC \leftarrow A;$$
$$SP--;$$

Fig. 2.12. The jump instructions **jump** and **jumpz** A

alternatively be used as jump targets. In this case, the jump targets are given relative to the code address of the jump instruction. This can be advantageous as smaller addresses would suffice to describe jump targets. Relative addresses also make it easier to *relocate* the code, that is to place it at any location in the code memory.

In order to specify the translation schemes, we find it convenient to introduce *symbolic labels* for instructions that are used as targets in jump instructions. Such a label stands for the address of the instruction that carries the label. In a second pass following code generation, the symbolic labels can be replaced by absolute instruction addresses.

We start with a one-sided conditional statement s of the form **if** (e) s'. Code generation for s places the code for evaluating e and s' consecutively into the program memory and additionally inserts jump instructions such that a correct control flow is guaranteed (Fig. 2.13). In case of one-sided conditionals, a conditional jump must be inserted following the code for evaluating the condition e. This jump branches to the instruction immediately *after* the code for statement s: If at run-time, the condi-

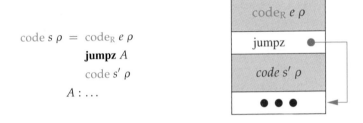

$$\text{code } s\,\rho \;=\; \text{code}_R\; e\,\rho$$
$$\textbf{jumpz } A$$
$$\text{code } s'\,\rho$$
$$A:\ldots$$

Fig. 2.13. Code generation for one-sided conditional statements

tion e is evaluated to 0, program execution immediately continues after the code for statement s. Otherwise, if the condition e evaluates to a value different from 0, the instruction sequence for the statement s' is executed.

We use the same strategy for the code generation for a two-sided conditional statement s of the form **if** (e) s_1 **else** s_2: the code sequences for e, s_1 and s_2 are consecutively placed in the program memory. In between suitable jumps are inserted to guarantee a correct control flow (Fig. 2.14). A conditional jump again follows the code for the condition e. The jump target is the beginning of the *else* block s_2. An *unconditional* jump is inserted immediately after the code for s_1. Its jump target is the first instruction after the code for statement s. This prevents the code for statement s_2 from being executed following the code for statement s_1.

Example 2.5.1 Assume that $\rho = \{x \mapsto 4, y \mapsto 7\}$ and consider the conditional statement s of the form:

$$\textbf{if } (x > y)$$
$$x \leftarrow x - y;$$
$$\textbf{else } y \leftarrow y - x;$$

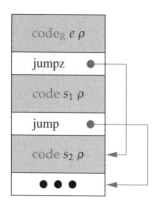

$$
\begin{aligned}
\text{code } s\, \rho = \quad & \text{code}_R\, e\, \rho \\
& \textbf{jumpz } A \\
& \text{code } s_1\, \rho \\
& \textbf{jump } B \\
A: \ & \text{code } s_2\, \rho \\
B: \ & \ldots
\end{aligned}
$$

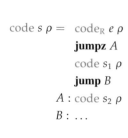

Fig. 2.14. Code generation for two-sided conditional statements

Then   code $s\, \rho$ results in:

loada 4	**loada** 4	*A:*	**loada** 7
loada 7	**loada** 7		**loada** 4
gr	**sub**		**sub**
jumpz *A*	**storea** 4		**storea** 7
	pop		**pop**
	jump *B*	*B:*	. . .

□

We now consider a *while* loop s of the form **while** $(e)\ s'$. The instruction sequence generated for s is shown in Fig. 2.15. A conditional jump to the first instruction after

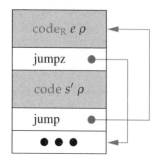

$$
\begin{aligned}
\text{code } s\, \rho = A: \ & \text{code}_R\, e\, \rho \\
& \textbf{jumpz } B \\
& \text{code } s'\, \rho \\
& \textbf{jump } A \\
B: \ & \ldots
\end{aligned}
$$

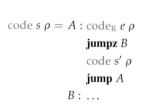

Fig. 2.15. Translation of a *while* loop

the loop is inserted immediately after the code for evaluating the condition e. At the end of the code for the loop body s' an unconditional jump back to the beginning of the code for the condition e is inserted.

Example 2.5.2 Assume that $\rho = \{a \mapsto 7, b \mapsto 8, c \mapsto 9\}$ is an address environment and s the statement:

$$\textbf{while } (a > 0) \; \{c \leftarrow c + 1; \; a \leftarrow a - b; \}$$

Then   code $s \, \rho$ produces the sequence:

A:	**loada** 7	**loada** 9	**loada** 7	B: . . .
	loadc 0	**loadc** 1	**loada** 8	
	gr	**add**	**sub**	
	jumpz B	**storea** 9	**storea** 7	
		pop	**pop**	
			jump A	

☐

Code generation may get more complicated if the body of the loop contains *break* or *continue* statements. A **break** can be interpreted as an unconditional jump to the first instruction following the loop. A **continue**, instead, only jumps to the end of the loop body, which means to the beginning of the code for the condition. Thus for correct code generation, the code function code additionally has to maintain the current jump targets for **break** or **continue**. For details we refer to Exercise 6.

A *for* loop s of the form **for** $(e_1; e_2; e_3) \; s'$ is equivalent to the following sequence of statements:

$$e_1; \; \textbf{while } (e_2) \; \{s' \; e_3; \}$$

provided that s' does not contain a *continue* statement. In this case, we translate:

$$
\begin{aligned}
\text{code } s \, \rho = \; &\text{code}_R \; e_1 \\
&\textbf{pop} \\
A : \; &\text{code}_R \; e_2 \; \rho \\
&\textbf{jumpz } B \\
&\text{code } s' \; \rho \\
&\text{code}_R \; e_3 \; \rho \\
&\textbf{pop} \\
&\textbf{jump } A \\
B : \; &\ldots
\end{aligned}
$$

In the presence of *continue* statements in the body s' of the loop, we proceed with the translation in a similar way. We only make sure that every **continue** in s' is interpreted as an unconditional jump to the end of s', that is, to the first instruction of the code for e_3 (if it exists).

Let us now turn to *switch* statements as provided by the programming language C. This statement is meant to efficiently support indexed jumps depending on the value of a selector expression. For simplicity, we assume that all occurring cases are from a range 0 to $k - 1$ for some constant k. All other values of the selection expression are supposed to jump to the *default* alternative. To simplify matters further, we assume that the cases are arranged in ascending order and each case is terminated with a **break**. Our *switch* statement s, thus, is of the form:

> **switch** (e) {
>> **case** 0: ss_0 **break**;
>> **case** 1: ss_1 **break**;
>>
>> $\vdots$
>>
>> **case** $k - 1$: ss_{k-1} **break**;
>> **default:** ss_k
>
> }

where ss_i are sequences of statements. *switch* statements can be translated by using *indexed jumps*. An indexed jump is a jump in which the jump target is computed at run-time. For that, we introduce the instruction **jumpi** B, which jumps to the sum of B and the value on top of the stack (Fig. 2.16). Then, the instruction sequence for

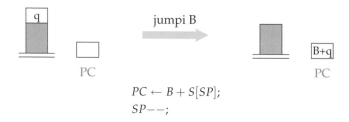

$$PC \leftarrow B + S[SP];$$
$$SP--;$$

Fig. 2.16. The indexed jump **jumpi** B

the *switch* statement s is given by:

code $s \, \rho$	=	code$_R$ $e \, \rho$		C_0:	code $ss_0 \, \rho$		B:	**jump** C_0
		check $0 \, k \, B$			**jump** D			$\ldots$
					$\ldots$			**jump** C_k
				C_k:	code $ss_k \, \rho$		D:	$\ldots$
					jump D			

The *macro* check $0 \; k \; B$ produces code for checking if the R-value of e lies in the interval $[0, k]$ and for performing an indexed jump. The table of possible jump targets is located at address B. The jump table contains direct jumps to the first instruction of each alternative. A jump to the first instruction immediately following the *switch* statement is inserted at the end of each alternative. The macro check could be implemented as follows:

check 0 k B	=	**dup**	**dup**		**jumpi** B
		loadc 0	**loadc** k	A :	**pop**
		geq	**leq**		**loadc** k
		jumpz A	**jumpz** A		**jumpi** B

The integer value on top of the stack, which is used for the case selection, is needed twice for comparing it with the lower and upper bound of the interval $[0, k - 1]$, respectively. Only if the selection value is from the interval $[0, k - 1]$ can it be used for indexing the jump table. The selection value must be *duplicated* before every comparison since every comparison in our virtual machine consumes the value. For this, we use the instruction **dup** (Fig. 2.17). The implementation of the macro is quite

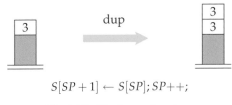

$$S[SP + 1] \leftarrow S[SP]; SP{+}{+};$$

Fig. 2.17. The instruction **dup**

straightforward. For values i in the interval $[0, k - 1]$, the target of the indexed jump is an unconditional jump to the start address of the i-th alternative. In contrast, if the R-value of e is smaller than 0 or larger than k, it is replaced with k before using it for the indexed jump. For this value k the target of the indexed jump is the unconditional jump to the *default* alternative.

In our translation scheme, the jump table is placed at the very end of the instruction sequence for the *switch* statement. As an alternative, it could have been placed directly after the macro check. This choice could have saved some unconditional jumps. Code generation may then, however, need further traversals over the statement in order to collect the start addresses of the different cases.

The translation scheme for the simplified *switch* statement can be generalized. If the smallest occurring value is u (instead of 0), the R-value of e is first decremented by u before using it as an index. A strictly ascending order of the selector values is not necessary. Some alternatives may not be terminated by **break**. Also gaps in the interval of possible cases can be tolerated. Then the missing entries of the jump table are filled with unconditional jumps to the beginning of the *default* alternative. Problems only arise if the interval of possible selector values is very large while at the same time few values are actually used. In Exercise 8 approaches can be developed to overcome such difficulties.

2.6 Memory Allocation for Variables of Basic Types

In this section we introduce some important concepts of compiler design, namely the concepts of *compile-time* and *run-time*, *static*, and *dynamic*. At *compile-time*, a given C program is compiled into a CMA program. At *run-time* this compiled C program is executed with input data. *Static* information about a C program is all information about this program that is known at compile-time or that can be computed or derived from other known information. *Dynamic* information is all information that only becomes available when executing the CMA program with the input data.

We have already seen examples of static and dynamic information about C programs. Static information includes, for instance, the target addresses of conditional or unconditional jumps, since they are, after all, computed from the source program with the aid of the code function. Obviously, this also holds true for all of the generated CMA program. Thus, the CMA program as a whole is static. In general, the values of variables and, thus, also the values of expressions containing variables, are dynamic. These values may depend on input values of the program, which become available only at run-time. Since the values of the conditions in statements are dynamic, the control flow after evaluating a condition is also dynamic.

Consider a list of variable declarations of a C program of the form:

$$t_1 \ x_1; \ldots; t_k \ x_k;$$

For the moment, let us assume that all types are basic. According to our assumption about the size of memory locations and the availability of memory, the values for each variable x_i of a basic type **int** or **float, char**, as well as enumeration types and pointer variables, can be stored in a single memory location. This means that we do not attempt, as is done in real compilers, to pack several small values into one word. We obtain thus a simple scheme for storage allocation. We assign consecutive addresses to variables in the order of their appearance in the list of declarations of the program. The addresses start at the beginning of the stack. For the moment we consider only programs without blocks and functions. The first assigned address is 1. For reasons that will become clear when we consider functions and blocks, the assigned addresses are called *relative addresses*. The absolute address 1, thus, is interpreted as the address 1 relative to the base address 0.

Let ρ denote a function that maps variables to their respective relative addresses. Our strategy of storage allocation then means that

$$\rho(x_i) = i \text{ for } 1 \leq i \leq k.$$

The relative addresses assigned in this way are static, since they result (in a simple way) from preprocessing the source program, namely, from the positions of the variables within the list of declarations.

These addresses are, of course, located in the memory area that has been reserved for the stack of the C-Machine. When we deal with functions and procedures, it will turn out that we are actually talking about several stacks, nested into each other. One is *large* and contains the data sections of all functions that have been called and not yet returned and, thus, grows or shrinks when a function is entered or exited, respectively. The others are *small* and accommodate, for each not yet terminated function, the intermediate values that are used during the evaluation of expressions. The assignment of memory locations, that is, addresses, to variables defines the structure of the data sections.

2.7 Memory Allocation for Arrays and Structures

The C programming language only provides *static arrays*. Consider the following declaration of an array a:

$$\textbf{int } a \; [11];$$

How many memory locations will be occupied by the array a? Obviously, a consists of the eleven elements:

$$a[0], \; a[1], \; a[2], \; a[3], \; a[4], \; a[5], \; a[6], \; a[7], \; a[8], \; a[9], \; a[10]$$

According to our assumptions, each element occupies one memory location. Thus, the array requires eleven memory locations for its elements. We place these elements consecutively into the stack and record in the address environment for a the start address, that is, the address of the element $a[0]$.

In general, the elements need not always be of basic type, but can themselves be composite. Therefore, we need an auxiliary function for constructing the memory allocation for composite variables. For each type t, this function determines the number of necessary memory locations:

$$|t| = \begin{cases} 1 & \text{if } t \text{ is basic} \\ k \cdot |t'| & \text{if } t \equiv t' \; [k] \end{cases}$$

This auxiliary function is provided in the C programming language through the library function sizeof.

Also in the presence of complex types such as array, we still place the declared variables consecutively in memory. For a sequence d of declarations of the form $t_1 \, x_1; \ldots; t_k \, x_k;$ we define the address environment ρ by:

$$\begin{aligned} \rho(x_1) &= 1 \\ \rho(x_i) &= \rho(x_{i-1}) + |t_{i-1}| \qquad \text{for } i > 1 \end{aligned}$$

We emphasize that this address environment can be computed at compile-time directly from the declaration d. Accordingly for storing value, say 42, into the element $a[0]$ of the array a, we could use the following sequence of instructions:

$$\textbf{loadc } 42; \; \textbf{loadc } \rho(a); \; \textbf{store}; \; \textbf{pop}$$

where the address $\rho(a)$ is statically known.

Code generation becomes more interesting for the assignment $a[i] \leftarrow 42$; where i is an *int* variable. The variable i gets its value only at run-time. Therefore, instructions must be generated that first compute the current value of i. Then, the corresponding element of the array is selected by adding the required offset to the start address $\rho(a)$:

loadc 42; **loadc** $\rho(a)$; **loadc** $\rho(i)$; **load**; **add**; **store**; **pop**

More generally, let a be an expression that represents an array of elements of type t. For determining the start address of the element $a[e]$, first the start address of the array a is determined. By computing the R-value of e, the index of the selected element is obtained. This index, scaled with the required space for each single element, is added to the start address of the array, in order to obtain the address of the location for the expression $a[e]$. Altogether, the value

$$(L\text{-}value\ of\ a) + |t| * (R\text{-}value\ of\ e)$$

is computed. In order to generate the corresponding code, we extend the code function code_L to indexed array expressions by:

$$
\begin{aligned}
\text{code}_L\ a[e]\ \rho \quad = \quad & \text{code}_L\ a\ \rho \\
& \text{code}_R\ e\ \rho \\
& \textbf{loadc}\ |t| \\
& \textbf{mul} \\
& \textbf{add}
\end{aligned}
$$

If the L-value of an indexed array expression $a[e]$ is known, the related R-value can be obtained by loading the contents of the addressed memory location. However, this only works if the elements of the indexed array fit exactly into one memory location. We will soon discuss how composite R-values can be dealt with.

First, we look at the problem of memory allocation and addressing of *aggregates* or *structures*. Let the aggregate variable x be declared by:

struct t {**int** a; **int** b; } x;

Then we assign the address of the first available memory location to the variable x, as before. The components of x *relative* obtain addresses relative to the start of the structure, such that $a \mapsto 0$, $b \mapsto 1$. These relative addresses depend only on the type t. We, thus, collect them in the function **offsets**, which assigns the suitable relative addresses to pairs (t, c) of aggregate types and their components.

More generally, let t be an aggregate type of the form **struct** $\{t_1\ c_1; \ldots t_k\ c_k; \}$. We define:

$$
\begin{aligned}
\text{offsets}(t, c_1) &= 0 \quad \text{and} \\
\text{offsets}(t, c_i) &= \text{offsets}(t, c_{i-1}) + |t_{i-1}| \quad \text{for } i > 1
\end{aligned}
$$

The size of the aggregate type t is the sum of the sizes of its components:

$$|t| = \sum_{i=1}^{k} |t_i|$$

The addressing of aggregate components is analogous to the addressing of elements in an array and consists of the following steps:

1. Load the start address of the aggregate;
2. Increment the address by the relative address of the member.

This produces the final address as a usable L-value. In general, let e be an expression of the aggregate type t, which has a member c. Then, the following code is generated for the computation of the L-value:

$$\mathrm{code}_L\ (e.c)\ \rho \quad = \quad \begin{array}{l} \mathrm{code}_L\ e\ \rho \\ \mathbf{loadc}\ m \\ \mathbf{add} \end{array}$$

where $m = \mathsf{offsets}(t, c)$. How is the R-value of a member obtained? For components whose type is composed, it is obviously not enough to load the contents of the addressed memory location. Instead, a whole block must be loaded onto the top of the stack. To deal with this situation, we generalize the instruction **load** to instructions **load** m for any non-negative value m. These instructions place at the top of the stack the contents of m consecutive memory locations, starting from the address currently on top of the stack (Fig. 2.18). In particular, the instruction **load** 1 is equivalent

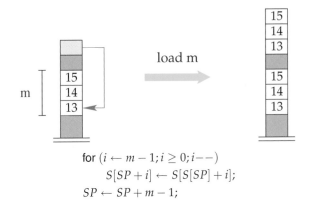

$$\mathbf{for}\ (i \leftarrow m - 1; i \geq 0; i--)$$
$$S[SP + i] \leftarrow S[S[SP] + i];$$
$$SP \leftarrow SP + m - 1;$$

Fig. 2.18. The instruction **load** m

to our previous instruction **load**. Thus, for computing the R-value of an expression e of an aggregate type of size m, we generate code by:

$$\mathrm{code}_R\ (e)\ \rho \quad = \quad \begin{array}{l} \mathrm{code}_L\ e\ \rho \\ \mathbf{load}\ m \end{array}$$

On purpose, we have restricted the applicability of this code scheme to expressions of aggregate types. Arrays are also composite types. For historical reasons, the R-value of an array a in C is *not* the sequence of R-values of its elements, but the *start address* of a. The reason is that, according to the C philosophy, the R-value of the array a is considered as a *pointer* to the memory area where the elements of a are located. The R-value of the array a is, thus, of the type $t *$, where t is the type of the elements of a. If e is an expression that represents an array, it follows:

$$\text{code}_R\ e\ \rho \quad = \quad \text{code}_L\ e\ \rho$$

We have already introduced how to load composed structures. But we need also the ability to store structures. For this, we generalize the instruction **store** to instructions **store** m for any non-negative value m (Fig. 2.19). The general form of the assignment

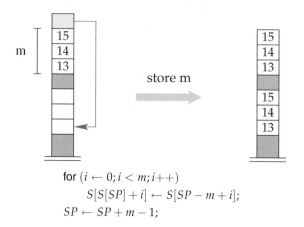

$$\text{for } (i \leftarrow 0; i < m; i++)$$
$$S[S[SP] + i] \leftarrow S[SP - m + i];$$
$$SP \leftarrow SP + m - 1;$$

Fig. 2.19. The instruction **store** m

of a value of aggregate type t is, thus:

$$\text{code}_R\ (e_1 \leftarrow e_2)\ \rho \quad = \quad \text{code}_R\ e_2\ \rho$$
$$\text{code}_L\ e_1\ \rho$$
$$\textbf{store } |t|$$

Of course, we allow ourselves the abbreviations:

$$\textbf{loada } q\ m \quad = \quad \textbf{loadc } q$$
$$\textbf{load } m$$

$$\textbf{storea } q\ m \quad = \quad \textbf{loadc } q$$
$$\textbf{store } m$$

As we can no longer assume that an expression always has an R-value of size 1, we must ensure that with a statement e; all m locations that belong to the value e are removed from the stack. Instead of a single instruction **pop**, we could simply insert m such instructions – or we could allow ourselves a new instruction **pop** m as an optimization. The implementation of this instruction is left to the reader.

2.8 Pointers and Dynamic Memory Allocation

In imperative programming languages, pointers and dynamic memory allocation for anonymous objects are closely related. So far, we have only considered memory allocation for variables that are introduced by declarations. In the declaration, a name is introduced for the object, and a static (relative) address is assigned to this name.

If a programming language supports pointers, these can be used to access objects without names. Linked data structures can be implemented by means of pointers. Their size may vary dynamically, and individual objects are not allocated by a declaration, but via a dynamic call to a memory allocator. The semantics of C are not very precise with respect to the *life-ranges* of dynamically allocated objects. The implementation of a programming language can deallocate the memory occupied by an object already before the end of its life-range without breaking the semantics, as long as it is guaranteed that program execution may no longer access the object. The task of freeing memory that is occupied by unreachable objects is called the *garbage collection*.

As briefly outlined in Sect. 2.1, data areas for the local variables of functions (and their organizational needs) is allocated in the lower end of the data region S when functions are entered and deallocated when functions are exited. This stack-style allocation and deallocation of memory does not match the life-ranges of dynamically allocated objects. Therefore, dynamically allocated objects are placed in a storage area called *heap*, which is located at the upper end of S. The heap grows toward the stack whenever an object is dynamically allocated (Fig. 2.20). A new register of the

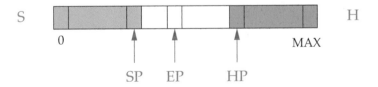

Fig. 2.20. The heap of the C-Machine

C-machine, the *Heap Pointer*, *HP*, points to the lowest occupied memory location in the heap. New objects on the heap are created by means of the instruction **new** (Fig. 2.21). The instruction **new** interprets the value on top of the stack as the size of the object to be created and replaces it with the start address of the memory block

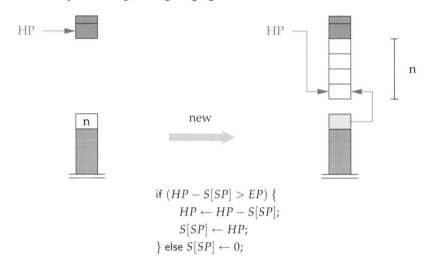

$$\text{if } (HP - S[SP] > EP) \{$$
$$\quad HP \leftarrow HP - S[SP];$$
$$\quad S[SP] \leftarrow HP;$$
$$\} \text{ else } S[SP] \leftarrow 0;$$

Fig. 2.21. The instruction **new**

of the newly allocated object. Beforehand, we check whether there is still enough free storage space available for the object to be created. If there is not enough space available, the instruction **new** returns the value 0 instead.

For checking whether a collision of stack and heap has occurred, it suffices to compare the registers *HP* and *SP*. In principle, such a comparison must be inserted at each change of the stack height. In order to avoid these comparisons, our C-Machine additionally provides the register *EP*, the Extreme Pointer (Fig. 2.20). This register is supposed to point to the highest stack location that the register *SP* may point to during the evaluation of the current function call. As shown in Exercise 11, the maximum number of stack locations necessary for the evaluation of each expression can be precomputed at compile-time. Therefore, the new value for *EP* can be computed from the *SP* when entering a function. A *stack overflow* is, thus, already detected when entering or when leaving a function call.

Computing with pointer values means to be able

- to *create* pointers, that is, to return references to specific objects in memory; as well as
- to *dereference* pointers, that is, to access memory locations via pointers.

Technically, a C pointer is nothing but a memory address. In C, there are two ways to produce pointers: with a call of the library function **malloc** or through the use of the address operator &. A call **malloc**(*e*) for an expression *e* computes the *R*-value *m* of *e* and returns the start address of a new memory region of size *m*. By means of the instruction **new**, we translate:

$$\text{code}_R(\textbf{malloc}\,(e))\,\rho = \text{code}_R\,e\,\rho$$
$$\textbf{new}$$

Note that a call to the **malloc** function never fails. If there is not enough space available for the new object, the call still returns an address value, namely the value 0. A thorough programmer will, therefore, always check the return value of a call to **malloc** against 0, detect and handle this error situation correctly.

The address operator & when applied to the expression e, returns a pointer to the storage object of e, that is, to the object of the type of e that is located at the start address of e. Thus, the R-value of the expression $\&e$ equals the L-value of the expression e:

$$\text{code}_R \ (\&e) \ \rho = \text{code}_L \ e \ \rho$$

Assume that e is an expression that evaluates to the pointer value p. This pointer value is the address of a memory object o. The memory object o can be accessed by *dereferencing* the pointer p, that is, by applying the prefix operator $*$. Since the R-value of e represents the L-value of $*e$, we define:

$$\text{code}_L \ (*e) \ \rho = \text{code}_R \ e \ \rho$$

An important feature of the programming language C is that it supports *pointer arithmetic*. That means that an *int* value a can be added to or subtracted from a pointer p. Pointer arithmetic is meant to support traversing sequences of similar memory objects by means of a pointer. If the pointer p points to a value of type t, then the expression $p + a$ represents a pointer to the a-th next memory object. This means for a sum $e_1 + e_2$ where e_1 is of type $t *$ and e_2 is of type **int**, the R-value of e_2 must first be scaled with $|t|$, before it can be added to the R-value of e_1. An analogous implicit scaling takes place at subtractions. Thus, we define in this case:

$$
\begin{aligned}
\text{code}_R \ (e_1 + e_2) \ \rho = \ &\text{code}_R \ e_1 \ \rho \\
&\text{code}_R \ e_2 \ \rho \\
&\textbf{loadc} \ |t| \\
&\textbf{mul} \\
&\textbf{add}
\end{aligned}
$$

$$
\begin{aligned}
\text{code}_R \ (e_1 - e_2) \ \rho = \ &\text{code}_R \ e_1 \ \rho \\
&\text{code}_R \ e_2 \ \rho \\
&\textbf{loadc} \ |t| \\
&\textbf{mul} \\
&\textbf{sub}
\end{aligned}
$$

As an application, we obtain a translation scheme for the expression $e_1[e_2]$ for an expression e_1 of type $t *$ and an *int* expression e_2. Since the indexed pointer expression is an abbreviation for the expression $*(e_1 + e_2)$, we obtain:

$$\text{code}_L \; e_1[e_2] \; \rho = \text{code}_L \; (*(e_1 + e_2)) \; \rho$$
$$= \text{code}_R \; (e_1 + e_2) \; \rho$$
$$= \text{code}_R \; e_1 \; \rho$$
$$\text{code}_R \; e_2 \; \rho$$
$$\textbf{loadc} \; |t|$$
$$\textbf{mul}$$
$$\textbf{add}$$

It is worth noting that this scheme is consistent with our scheme for array indexing. If the expression e_1 defines an array, the L-value of e_1 would have been used instead of the R-value as in the case of references. Since for arrays, the L-value and the R-value agree, our compilation scheme can be used both for indexed accesses for references and for arrays.

At the end of this section, we consider a slightly larger example where several translation schemes are applied.

Example 2.8.1 For a declaration:

$$\textbf{struct } t \; \{ \; \textbf{int } a[7]; \textbf{struct } t *b; \; \};$$
$$\textbf{int } i, j;$$
$$\textbf{struct } t *pt;$$

the expression $e \; \equiv \; ((pt \to b) \to a)[i + 1]$ is to be translated. Here, the operator $\to$ is an abbreviation for a dereference followed by a selection. This means:

$$e \to c \quad \equiv \quad (*e).c$$

If e has type $t *$ for a structure t with a member c, we therefore obtain for $m = \text{offsets}(t, c)$:

$$\text{code}_L \; (e \to c) \; \rho = \text{code}_L \; ((*e).c) \; \rho$$
$$= \text{code}_L \; (*e) \; \rho$$
$$\textbf{loadc } m$$
$$\textbf{add}$$
$$= \text{code}_R \; e \; \rho$$
$$\textbf{loadc } m$$
$$\textbf{add}$$

In our example, we have $\text{offsets}(t, a) = 0$, and $\text{offsets}(t, b) = 7$. Let us assume that we are given an address environment

$$\rho = \{ i \mapsto 1, j \mapsto 2, pt \mapsto 3 \}$$

Then, the resulting code for the expression e is:

$$\text{code}_L \; e \; \rho \quad = \quad \begin{array}{l} \text{code}_L \left((pt \to b) \to a \right) \rho \\ \text{code}_R \; (i+1) \; \rho \\ \textbf{loadc } 1 \\ \textbf{mul} \\ \textbf{add} \end{array} \quad = \quad \begin{array}{l} \text{code}_L \left((pt \to b) \to a \right) \rho \\ \textbf{loada } 1 \\ \textbf{loadc } 1 \\ \textbf{add} \\ \textbf{loadc } 1 \\ \textbf{mul} \\ \textbf{add} \end{array}$$

where:

$$\text{code}_L \left((pt \to b) \to a \right) \rho \quad = \quad \begin{array}{l} \text{code}_R \; (pt \to b) \; \rho \\ \textbf{loadc } 0 \\ \textbf{add} \end{array} \quad = \quad \begin{array}{l} \textbf{loada } 3 \\ \textbf{loadc } 7 \\ \textbf{add} \\ \textbf{load} \\ \textbf{loadc } 0 \\ \textbf{add} \end{array}$$

Altogether we obtain the sequence:

loada 3	**load**	**loada** 1	**loadc** 1
loadc 7	**loadc** 0	**loadc** 1	**mul**
add	**add**	**add**	**add**

This sequence could not as easily be derived by hand without systematically applying the translation schemes. We also observe that our schemes still leave room for
various optimizations. For instance, additions of 0 could have been saved as well as
multiplications by 1. These inefficiencies could have been avoided directly during
code generation, by introducing appropriate compilation schemes for special cases.
To keep the schemes clear, we did not follow this option. Instead, we rely on a post-
pass optimizer to carry out these local code improvements separately.   □

The translation schemes for pointer expressions are now complete. What remains
open is the question of how to implement the explicit *release* of memory blocks.
Releasing the memory block pointed to by a pointer is problematic, because other
pointers still might point into this memory block. Such pointers would after the release be called *dangling*.

Even if we assume that the programmer always knows what she is doing, the
heap could become *fragmented* after several releases, as shown in Fig. 2.22. The free
memory regions can be scattered quite unevenly over the heap. There are various
techniques for reusing these regions during program execution. In any case, further
data structures are required by the run-time system for this purpose. Their adminis-
tration increases the cost of calls to the functions **malloc** or **free**.

In our minimal compiler, we follow a different strategy: we ignore releases of
memory. This implementation strategy is obviously correct. If it is not necessarily

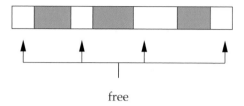

free

Fig. 2.22. The heap after the release of several memory blocks

optimal w.r.t. consumption of memory space, it is at least simple. Accordingly, we translate:

$$\text{code}\ (\mathbf{free}\ (e);\ )\ \rho\quad=\quad\text{code}_R\ e\ \rho$$
$$\mathbf{pop}$$

2.9 Functions

As a preparation for the translation of functions, we briefly recall the related concepts, terms, and problems. The *declaration* of a function consists of:

- a name by which it can be called,
- the specification of the type of the return value,
- the specification of the formal parameters, which, together with the type for the return value, form the input and output interface,
- a function *body*, which consists of a sequence of local declarations and statements.

If the function does not return a value, that is, if it is a *procedure*, the type of the return value is specified as **void**.

A function is *called*, or invoked, when it is applied to actual parameter values within the statement part of another function. A called function may itself call other functions, including itself. When a called function f has executed all its statements, it *returns*, and the caller, that is the function that invoked f, continues execution immediately after the call.

All function calls that occur during the execution of a program can be organized into an ordered tree, the *call tree* of the program execution. Each node in the call tree is labeled with a function name. The root of the call tree is labeled with the name of the function *main*, whose call starts program execution. If a node is labeled with a function name f, the sequence of its direct successors consists of the functions successively invoked when executing the body of f. The label f may occur multiple times in the call tree; to be precise, it occurs as often as f is called during this execution of the program. We call each occurrence of f an *incarnation* of f. An incarnation is characterized by the path from the root of the tree to the node. We call this path the *incarnation path* of an incarnation of f.

Consider the state of program execution when a certain incarnation of f is active. All predecessors of this incarnation, that is, all nodes on the incarnation path, have already been called, but have not yet returned. We say that all these incarnations are at this moment *live*.

Example 2.9.1 Consider the C program:

```
int n;

int fac(int n) {
    if (n ≤ 0) return 1;
    else return n * fac(n − 1);
}
```

```
int main() {
    int r;
    n ← 2;
    r ← fac(n) + fac(n − 1);
    return r;
}
```

Figure 2.23 shows the call tree for this program. The arrow points to the second

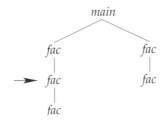

Fig. 2.23. The call tree for the example program

recursive call of the function *fac*. At this moment the main function *main* and two recursive calls of *fac* are live. □

Programs may have different program executions since they depend on input. Accordingly, there can be more than one call tree for a given program p. Since the number of different executions of p may be infinite, there can also be infinitely many different call trees for p.

A name can occur multiple times in a program. A *defining occurrence* of a name is an occurrence in a declaration or in a formal parameter list where it is defined. All other occurrences are called *applied occurrences*.

Consider the names occurring in functions. The names that are introduced as formal parameters or via local declarations are called *local*. When a function is called, new *incarnations* are created for all local names. Space is allocated for each variable according to the types specified in the declaration and (if necessary) filled with an initial value. In particular, the formal parameters receive the values of the actual parameters. The *life-range* of the created variable incarnation is equal to the life-range of the incarnation of the function. Therefore, the space occupied by locals can be released when returning from the function.[1] This behavior can be realized with

---

[1] These should be distinguished from *static* variables which are declared local to the given function f, but global to any incarnation of f.

a stack-style memory management. Accordingly, the stack frame that was allocated for formal parameters, for locally declared variables, and for intermediate values (see Fig. 2.24) when entering the function is released when returning from the function.

Dealing with applied occurrences of names that are non-local is not as straightforward. These names are *global* with respect to the given function or block. The *visibility* and/or *scope rules* of the programming language determine how to find, for a given applied occurrence of a name, the corresponding defining occurrence. The dual, but equivalent, perspective is to identify for a given defining occurrence of a name x, all program locations where applied occurrences of x refer to the given defining occurrence.

From languages like ALGOL we know the following visibility rule: a defining occurrence of a name is visible in the *program unit* directly containing the declaration or specification minus all contained program units that introduce a new definition of this name. Here, *program unit* stands for a function or a *block*. Blocks are considered in Exercise 12.

Based on the given visibility rule, we reconsider the problem of establishing a relationship between defining and applied occurrences. When searching for the defining occurrence of a given applied occurrence of a name x, we start in the declaration part of the immediate program unit wherein the applied occurrence of x occurs. If no defining occurrence of x is found there, we continue with the enclosing program unit, and so forth. If no defining occurrence can be found in all enclosing program units, including the whole program, then a programming error is encountered.

The dual approach is to start from a defining occurrence of x and then search the corresponding program unit for all occurring applied occurrences of x. This scan is blocked for program units that introduce new definitions of x.

Example 2.9.2 Consider the program from Example 2.9.1. The variable n is defined outside all functions and therefore is global with respect to function *main*. As the formal parameter of function *fac* is also named n, this global variable is not visible inside the function body. The applied occurrences of n within the body of *fac* therefore refer to the formal parameter of *fac*.   □

The given visibility rule corresponds to *static* scoping. Static scoping means that applied occurrences of names that are global to a program unit refer to the defining occurrences occurring in *textually* enclosing program units. The corresponding binding of names is static as it depends only on the program itself and not on the (dynamic) execution of the program. Every use of the global name x at run-time refers to the same incarnation of the statically bound defining occurrence of x.

In contrast, *dynamic scoping* means that an access to a global name is bound to the last created incarnation of this name – regardless of the function in which the name is defined. Static scoping is standard for all ALGOL-like languages and also for modern functional languages, such as HASKELL and OCAML, while older dialects of LISP use dynamic scoping.

Example 2.9.3 Consider the following program:

$$\begin{array}{ll}
\textbf{int } x \leftarrow 1; & \textbf{int } main() \, \{ \\
\textbf{void } q() \, \{ & \quad \textbf{int } x \leftarrow 2; \\
\quad printf\,("\%d", x); & \quad q(); \\
\} & \}
\end{array}$$

With static scoping, the applied occurrence of the variable x in function q refers to the global variable x. Therefore, the value 1 is printed. In contrast, the dynamically last defining occurrence of the variable x before the call to function q is the one in the function *main*. With dynamic scoping, the value of the applied occurrence of x that is printed in q is 2. □

In contrast to PASCAL, the programming language ANSI-C does not allow nested function definitions. This design decision greatly simplifies the treatment of visibility. For ANSI-C, it suffices to distinguish between two kinds of variables: *global* variables, which are declared outside of function definitions, and *local* or (in C jargon) *automatic* variables, which are defined local to particular functions.

2.9.1 Memory Organization of the C-Machine

In the following, we describe the organization of the memory area for maintaining the sequence of live incarnations of functions. This part of S is the *run-time stack* of the CMA. The run-time stack consists of a sequence of *stack frames*, one for each live incarnation of a function, in the same order in which these appear in the incarnation path. In order to efficiently support returns from functions, the stack frames are linked together. Each stack frame for the incarnation of a function f contains a reference to the stack frame of the incarnation of the function g that invoked f. This incarnation of g is called the *dynamic predecessor* of f.

The stack frame corresponding to an incarnation of f is allocated when f is called. The organization of a stack frame of the C-Machine is shown in Fig. 2.24. We introduce a further register, the *Frame Pointer*, *FP*, which points to a well-defined place in the current stack frame. In the stack frame, further space is allocated for storing registers whose contents must be saved when entering a function and restored when returning from the call. In the C-Machine these are the registers *PC*, *FP*, and *EP*. The saved value of *PC* is the *return address* from where program execution is supposed to resume when the function call is completed. The saved value of *FP* is the link to the stack frame of the calling function, that is the *dynamic predecessor* of the current function call. Finally, the value of *EP* must be saved because it is only valid for the current call.

The locations where these three register are saved are called the *organizational cells*, because they assist in organizing the start and end of functions correctly and efficiently. The organizational cells form a section within the stack frame of the current function incarnation. In this stack frame, we allocate the formal parameters and local variables of the current function. This allows us to access these variables relative to the Frame Pointer *FP* with *fixed relative addresses*. If the Frame Pointer points to

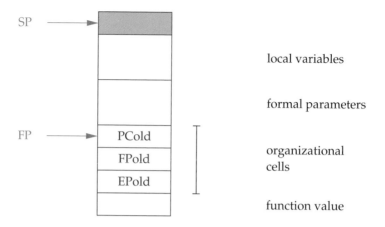

Fig. 2.24. A stack frame of the C Machine

the top organizational cell (that is, the saved *PC*), positive relative addresses, starting with 1, can be assigned to the local variables.

Above the data section, we allocate the *local stack*, that is, the stack that we introduced in Sect. 2.2 for the evaluation of expressions. The maximal height of this local stack can also be statically determined (see Exercise 11).

Conceptually, two more things must be allocated in the stack frame, the actual parameters and the return value of the function. With the actual parameters we have a problem: the programming language C allows the definition of functions with *variable-length* parameter lists, such as the function *printf*, whose first parameter is mandatory, while the number of further actual parameters only becomes evident from the call. Within such a function, code generation may only assume that the mandatory parameters are available. In order to assign fixed relative addresses also for these parameters, we use a trick: the actual parameters are placed on the stack *below* the organizational cells and in *reverse order*! In this way, the first parameter is placed on top of the second and so on. Relative addresses therefore are now *negative numbers* starting from -3. If the first parameter, for example, has size m, then it receives the relative address $-(m-2)$.

If the function returns a value, we should reserve a canonical place for it where it can be accessed with a fixed address relative to *FP*. We could introduce a separate section of the stack for the return value. After the return from the function call, though, the space for the actual parameters is no longer needed. Therefore, we choose to reuse this section for storing the return value.

2.9.2 Dealing with Local Variables

In Sects. 2.6 and 2.7, we described how to assign memory locations, that is, addresses, to names defined in declaration lists. There, we only considered programs with one list of declarations and one list of statements. In the absence of function definitions, it was not necessary to distinguish between global and local variables. In fact, we used *absolute addressing* for accessing variables, that is, variables were accessed relative to the start address of the memory area S.

An address environment assigns (relative) addresses to names. For a real C program, a name may also identify a function. The address assigned to a function f should be the (absolute) start address of the *code* for f in the program store C.

With formal parameters and local variables, on the other hand, we wish to access their incarnations in the current function call. The addressing in this case is relative to the Frame Pointer FP. In order to distinguish these different modes of addressing, we extend the address environment ρ in such a way that ρ maintains, for each defined occurrence of a name, not only a relative address, but also the information of whether the name is global or local. The address environment ρ, thus, has now the functionality:

$$\rho : Names \rightarrow \{G, L\} \times \mathbb{Z}$$

where the tags G and L identify global or local scope, respectively. To allow access relative to the FP for local variables or formal parameters, it is enough to generalize the code function $code_L$ for names. For $\rho(x) = (tag, j)$ we now define:

$$code_L \; x \; \rho = \begin{cases} \textbf{loadc } j & \text{for the tag } G \\ \textbf{loadrc } j & \text{for the tag } L \end{cases}$$

The new instructions **loadrc** j push the value $FP + j$ on top of the stack (Fig. 2.25). As an optimization we again introduce special instructions for frequently occurring

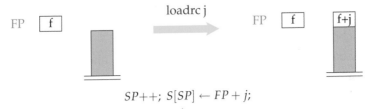

$$SP{+}{+}; \; S[SP] \leftarrow FP + j;$$

Fig. 2.25. The instruction **loadrc** j

instruction sequences:

$$\textbf{loadr } j \; m = \textbf{loadrc } j$$
$$\textbf{load } m$$

$$\textbf{storer } j \; m = \textbf{loadrc } j$$
$$\textbf{store } m$$

where we also write **loadr** j and **storer** j for **loadr** j 1 and **storer** j 1, respectively.

With this change, we can apply the translation schemes, which we developed step by step in the last sections, also to the bodies of functions. We only must additionally supply the address environment ρ_f at the entry point of a function f. In particular, we must ensure that the address environment provides the correct bindings for the visible names whenever it is used.

For processing a global variable declaration, we define a function elab_global. This function takes a pair (ρ, n) of an address environment ρ and a first available relative address n, together with a declaration $d \equiv t\ x$, and produces an extended address environment together with the next available relative address. We define:

$$\text{elab\_global}\ (\rho, n)\ (d)\ = (\rho \oplus \{x \mapsto (G, n)\}, n + |t|)$$

The expression $\rho \oplus \{x \mapsto a\}$ denotes the (partial) function obtained from ρ by adding for the argument x the value a. If ρ is already defined for x, then the old value in ρ for x is overwritten with the new value a.

Analogously, we define functions elab_formal and elab_local for processing declarations of formal parameters and local variables, respectively:

$$\text{elab\_formal}\ (\rho, z)\ (t\ x) = (\rho \oplus \{x \mapsto (L, z - |t|)\}, z - |t|)$$
$$\text{elab\_local}\ (\rho, n)\ (t\ x)\ = (\rho \oplus \{x \mapsto (L, n)\}, n + |t|)$$

The function elab_local is analogous to the function elab_global for processing declarations of global variables – the one difference is that now, instead of the tag G, the tag L is assigned. In contrast, we must be careful when defining the function elab_formal. Every further parameter must receive a *smaller* address. Instead of the first available relative address, we assign to the next parameter the lowest location z occupied so far by the stack frame, minus the size of the type of the variable.

By using these functions repeatedly, we can process lists of global variables, formal parameters, and local variables, respectively:

$$
\begin{aligned}
\text{elab\_globals}(\rho, n)\ ()\quad &= (\rho, n) \\
\text{elab\_globals}(\rho, n)\ (t\ x; ll) &= \text{elab\_globals}\ (\text{elab\_global}\ (\rho, n)\ (t\ x))\ (ll) \\
\text{elab\_formals}\ (\rho, z)\ ()\quad &= (\rho, z) \\
\text{elab\_formals}\ (\rho, z)\ (t\ x, dd) &= \text{elab\_formals}\ (\text{elab\_formal}\ (\rho, z)\ (t\ x))\ (dd) \\[4pt]
\text{elab\_locals}(\rho, n)\ ()\quad &= (\rho, n) \\
\text{elab\_locals}(\rho, n)\ (t\ x; ll)\ &= \text{elab\_locals}\ (\text{elab\_local}\ (\rho, n)\ (t\ x))\ (ll)
\end{aligned}
$$

Assume that we are given a function f without return value with lists dd and ll of declarations of formal parameters and local variables, respectively. From an address environment ρ for global names we obtain, thus, as address environment ρ_f for the function f:

$$\rho_f = \quad \text{let } \rho = \rho \oplus \{f \mapsto (G, \_f)\}$$
$$\text{in let } (\rho, \_) = \text{elab\_formals } (\rho, -2) \; dd$$
$$\text{in let } (\rho, \_) = \text{elab\_locals } (\rho, 1) \; ll$$
$$\text{in} \quad \rho$$

where $\_f$ identifies the start address of the code for f.

If the function f has a return value, we also remember in the address environment ρ_f for f the relative address in the stack frame where the return value is stored. For this we introduce a local auxiliary variable ret. Let t be the type of the return value and m be the space requirement of the mandatory formal parameters.

- We can place the return type at the lower boundary of the section for the formals, that is, from relative address $-(m+2)$ onwards if $|t| \le m$. For this, we expand our definition of ρ_f with the binding $\text{ret} \mapsto (L, -(m+2))$.
- A larger section is required for the return value than for the mandatory parameters if $|t| > m$. In this case, the return value is allocated from address $-(|t|+2)$ onwards. Thus, we add to ρ_f the binding $\text{ret} \mapsto (L, -(|t|+2))$.

Example 2.9.4 Consider again the C program of Example 2.9.1. As global names, we have n for a global variable together with fac and $main$ for functions. Then

$$\rho_0 = \{n \mapsto (G, 1)\}$$

is the address environment of global names known when processing the declarations of the function fac. From this address environment, we obtain the address environment ρ_{fac} within fac, by first adding the binding $fac \mapsto (G, \_fac)$ to ρ_0. Then, we record the binding $n \mapsto (L, 3)$ for the formal parameter n, which replaces the binding for the corresponding global variable. Finally, we add the relative address of the return value, which is -3. Thus, we obtain:

$$\rho_{fac} = \{fac \mapsto (G, \_fac), n \mapsto (L, 3), \text{ret} \mapsto (L, -3)\}$$

The name of the function fac is known already before the definition of the function $main$. Thus,

$$\rho_1 = \{n \mapsto (G, 1), fac \mapsto (G, \_fac)\}$$

With respect to this environment, the address environment ρ_{main} inside the function $main$ is given by:

$$\rho_{main} = \{fac \mapsto (G, \_fac), main \mapsto (G, \_main),$$
$$n \mapsto (G, 1), r \mapsto (L, 1), \text{ret} \mapsto (L, -3)\}$$

Even though the function $main$ does not have formal parameters, it does have a return value of size 1. As in the function fac, this value receives the relative address -3. In contrast to the function fac, the global variable n is not hidden in function $main$ by a formal parameter with the same name. Instead, ρ_{main} contains a binding for the additional local variable r as well as a binding for the global function name $main$.
□

2.9.3 Function Call and Return

Let us discuss the two crucial problems with the implementation of C functions, the call and, thus, starting the execution of a function and the return, that is, exiting after having processed a function's body.

First we examine the call of a function. Let f be the currently active function. Its stack frame is at the top of the stack. Now assume that function f calls a function g. An instruction sequence must be generated for the call of g that processes the call of g and leaves the return value on top of the stack. Note that this instruction sequence computes an R-value (as long as the function does not return **void**). In particular, this return value has no (sensible) L-value. This means that according to our translation schemes the return value cannot be directly accessed by a selector. One solution to this problem is to apply a program transformation before code generation that places the return values of all problematic function calls in auxiliary local variables. As an example, the assignment $x \leftarrow f(y + 2).a$; is transformed into the block:

$$\{ \textbf{struct } t \; tmp; \; tmp \leftarrow f(y+2); \; x \leftarrow tmp.a; \}$$

for a new variable tmp, where t is the return value of function f.

The following sequence of actions must be executed for starting the execution of the function g:

1. The values of the actual parameters must be computed and pushed onto the stack.
2. The old values of registers EP and FP must be pushed onto the stack.
3. The start address of function g must be computed.
4. The return address must be computed and recorded in the corresponding organizational cell.
5. Register FP must be made to point to the top of the new stack frame.
6. Control must proceed to the start address of g.
7. Register EP for the new call must be set to the current value of g.
8. Space must be reserved on the stack for the local variables of g.

Then the sequence of instructions for the body of function g can be executed. When designing translation schemes, we must distribute the listed actions among the caller f and the callee g. Such a distribution must take the respective knowledge into account. It is, for example, only the caller f that can provide the values of the actual parameters, while only function g knows the space requirement for its local variables. In our list, the borderline between caller code and callee code lies between points (6) and (7). For saving the registers EP and FP in point (2), we introduce the instruction **mark** (Fig. 2.26). This instruction pushes the contents of both registers consecutively onto the stack. For setting the new FP, saving the return address, and jumping to the code of the callee in points (6), (4) and (5), we introduce the instruction **call** (Fig. 2.27). The instruction **call** is the last instruction of the call sequence of g in the caller f. When executing this instruction, the PC register corresponds exactly to the return address! This means that the actions (4) and (5) are jointly implemented by swapping the contents of the topmost stack cell with the contents of register PS.

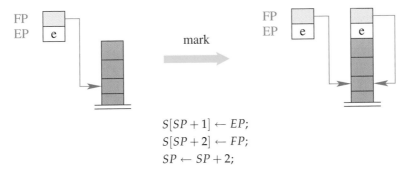

$$S[SP+1] \leftarrow EP;$$
$$S[SP+2] \leftarrow FP;$$
$$SP \leftarrow SP+2;$$

Fig. 2.26. The instruction **mark**

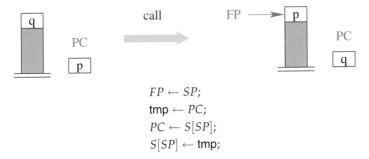

$$FP \leftarrow SP;$$
$$\text{tmp} \leftarrow PC;$$
$$PC \leftarrow S[SP];$$
$$S[SP] \leftarrow \text{tmp};$$

Fig. 2.27. The instruction **call**

Only actions (7) and (8) remain. We set the new EP relative to the current SP with the help of an instruction **enter** m where m is the total number of stack locations required inside the called function (Fig. 2.28). This instruction checks whether there

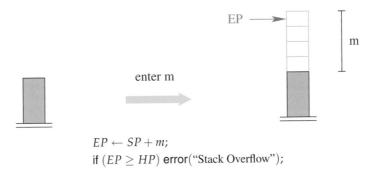

$$EP \leftarrow SP+m;$$
$$\text{if } (EP \geq HP) \text{ error(“Stack Overflow”)};$$

Fig. 2.28. The instruction **enter** m

is enough space on the stack for executing the current call. If this is not the case, program execution is aborted with an error message.

Finally, allocating m memory locations for the local variables is implemented by incrementing the register SP with m. This increment is realized by the instruction **alloc** m (Fig. 2.29). In particular, **alloc** 0 has no effect.

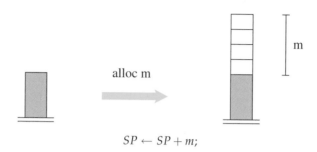

$$SP \leftarrow SP + m;$$

Fig. 2.29. The instruction **alloc** m

The instruction *alloc* m can also be used for allocating stack space for the return value of the function, in case that the space for the actual parameters is not sufficient. We now provide a translation scheme for a function call e of the form $g(e_1, \ldots, e_n)$. Let t be the return type of g, m the space requirement of the formal parameters, and $m' \geq m$ the space requirement of the actual parameters. Then we define:

$$
\begin{aligned}
\mathrm{code}_R \, e \, \rho = {} & \textbf{alloc } q \\
& \mathrm{code}_R \, e_n \, \rho \\
& \ldots \\
& \mathrm{code}_R \, e_1 \, \rho \\
& \textbf{mark} \\
& \mathrm{code}_R \, g \, \rho \\
& \textbf{slide } q' \, |t| \qquad \text{where} \\
& q \ = \mathsf{max}\,(|t| - m', 0) \\
& q' = \mathsf{if}\,(|t| \leq m)\; m' - m \\
& \qquad \textbf{else } \mathsf{max}\,(m' - |t|, 0)
\end{aligned}
$$

First, enough space is allocated to accommodate the return value below the organizational cells. If the return value is not located at the lower boundary of the stack frame, it must be moved down after the call. This is realized by the instruction **slide** q m (Fig. 2.30).

According to our translation scheme, the first argument of the second *slide* instruction is 0, whenever the function has no optional parameters. One can show that it is never necessary to simultaneously move results after and allocate additional stack space before the call.

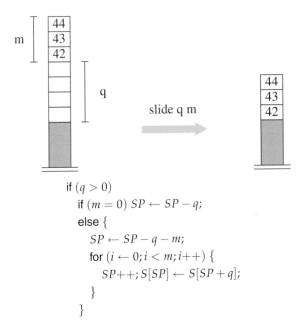

```
if (q > 0)
    if (m = 0) SP ← SP − q;
    else {
        SP ← SP − q − m;
        for (i ← 0; i < m; i++) {
            SP++; S[SP] ← S[SP + q];
        }
    }
```

Fig. 2.30. The instruction **slide** q m

Our scheme generates code for each actual parameter e_i which computes the R-value of e_i in the address environment ρ. This is consistent with passing parameters to the function *by value*. Other imperative programming languages, such as PASCAL or C++, also support parameter passing *by reference*. If the formal parameter x is a reference parameter, the L-value of the actual parameter is passed to x, instead of the R-value. Each access to the formal parameter x in the body of the function requires an *indirection* through the relative address of x. For a reference parameter x, we therefore modify the computation of the L-value of x to:

$$\text{code}_L\ x\ \rho\ =\ \textbf{loadr}\ \rho(x)$$

For the expression g which evaluates to the function to be called, code is generated for computing the R-value. This scheme allows us to call functions through pointers. In C, a function name is considered as a *reference* whose R-value equals its L-value:

$$\text{code}_R\ f\ \rho\ =\ \text{code}_L\ f\ \rho\ =\ \textbf{loadc}\ \rho(f)$$

Example 2.9.5 Consider the recursive function call $fac(n − 1)$ in the program of Example 2.9.1. Then, our translation scheme generates the instruction sequence:

alloc 0; **loadr** −3; **loadc** 1; **sub**; **mark**; **loadc** _fac; **call**; **slide** 0 1;

□

After having thoroughly examined the actions taken when entering a function, we now turn to the actions that are executed when exiting a function. These are:

1. (possibly) saving the return value,
2. recovering the registers EP and FP,
3. cleaning up the stack and jumping back to the code of the caller.

These actions can be executed entirely by the called function. Since we manage the start address of the return value – if it exists – in the address environment, saving the return value can be treated as an assignment. The other two tasks can be merged into the instruction **return** q (Fig. 2.31). Here, the constant q equals the number of

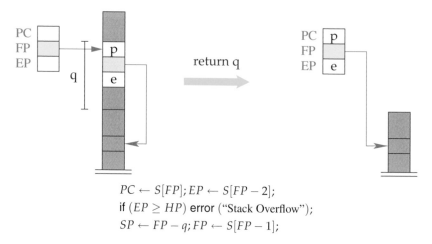

$$PC \leftarrow S[FP]; EP \leftarrow S[FP-2];$$
$$\text{if } (EP \geq HP) \text{ error (“Stack Overflow”)};$$
$$SP \leftarrow FP - q; FP \leftarrow S[FP-1];$$

Fig. 2.31. The instruction **return** q

cells above the return value that are supposed to be removed. A test for a collision between stack and heap must be performed before restoring the EP since the heap pointer might have been decreased during the function call. Program execution is aborted with an error message if the value of the EP, which is to be restored, is not smaller than the current value of HP.

Accordingly, the C statements **return;** and **return** e; for an expression e of type t are translated as follows:

$$\text{code } (\textbf{return;}) \, \rho = \textbf{return} \, (m+3)$$

$$\text{code } (\textbf{return } e;) \, \rho = \text{code}_R \, e \, \rho$$
$$\textbf{storer } \rho(\text{ret}) \, |t|$$
$$\textbf{return } q \qquad \text{where}$$
$$q = 3 + \max\{m - |t|, 0\}$$

where m is the space requirement of the function for all its formal parameters. Overall, the definition d of a function f of the form:

$$t\ f\ (params)\ \{locals\ ss\ \}$$

with return type t, declaration of formal parameters *params*, declaration of local variables *locals*, and statements sequence ss, is translated as follows:

$$\text{code } d\ \rho = \quad \_f: \quad \textbf{enter } k$$
$$\textbf{alloc } l$$
$$\text{code } ss\ \rho_f$$
$$\textbf{return } q$$

where k is the maximal space requirement for a call to function f, l is the number of memory locations for the local variables, ρ_f is the address environment for f, which is obtained from ρ along with *params*, *locals* as well as the size of the return type t, and $q = \max\{m - |t|, 0\}$, if m is the space requirement for the mandatory formal parameters.

Example 2.9.6 The definition of the function *fac* of Example 2.9.1 is translated into:

_fac:	**enter** q	**loadc** 1	A:	**loadr** -3		**mul**
	loadr -3	**storer** -3		**loadr** -3		**storer** -3
	loadc 0	**return** 3		**loadc** 1		**return** 3
	leq	**jump** B		**sub**		
	jumpz A			**mark**	B:	**return** 3
				loadc _fac		
				call		

Here, we have omitted the instructions **alloc** 0 and **slide** 0 1. Also note that the jump with address B is not reachable and, thus, can safely be removed.   □

2.10 Translation of Programs

It remains to specify how a complete C program p should be translated. For that, we assume that the value of the Heap Pointer, HP, before program execution is the largest memory address $+1$ and all other registers have the value 0. In particular, this means that the execution of the CMA program for p starts with the instruction in $C[0]$.

The program p is a sequence of declarations of global variables and functions, one of which defines the function **int** *main*(). Note that, for simplicity, we do not consider command line parameters for the function *main*. The code for program p, thus, consists of:

- code for the allocation of global variables;
- code for the function definitions;
- code for the call of function *main*;
- the instruction **halt**, to terminate program execution.

For simplicity, we assume that the variable declarations in p appear before the function declarations. Program p, thus, has the form:

$$dd\ df_1 \ldots df_n$$

where dd is a sequence of variable declarations and $df_1, \ldots, df_n$ are respectively the declarations of functions $f_1, \ldots, f_n$ with $f_n \equiv main$. Assume that $\emptyset$ identifies the empty address environment. Then

$$(\rho_0, k) = \textsf{elab\_globals}\ (1, \emptyset)\ dd$$

is the pair consisting of the address environment for the global variables of p and the first free relative address. If $\_f_i$ is the start address of function f_i, then the address environment before execution of the i-th function definition is given by:

$$\rho_i = \rho_{i-1} \oplus \{f_i \mapsto \_f_i\} \qquad (i = 1, \ldots, n)$$

We obtain the following translation scheme for p:

$$
\begin{array}{rcl}
\text{code } p & = & \textbf{enter } (k+3) \\
& & \textbf{alloc } k \\
& & \textbf{mark} \\
& & \textbf{loadc } \_f_n \\
& & \textbf{call} \\
& & \textbf{slide } (k-1)\ 1 \\
& & \textbf{halt} \\
\_f_1: & & \text{code } df_1\ \rho_1 \\
& & \vdots \\
\_f_n: & & \text{code } df_n\ \rho_n
\end{array}
$$

Before the call to the main function f_n, a total of $(k-1)$ memory cells for globals are allocated on top of the (forbidden) memory location with address 0. One more cell is reserved for the return value of f_n. Since SP has the value 0 before program execution, SP must be incremented by k. When executing the instruction **call**, a total of 3 further memory cells have been allocated on the stack. Accordingly, the instruction *enter* at program start must set the register EP to $SP + k + 3 = k + 3$. The return value of the initial call to *main* is placed in the memory location with address k. The instruction **halt**, which is supposed to return control to the operating system, does not know about globals and therefore expects the return value in a specific memory location, say with address 1. Therefore, the return value after the call is slid downwards by $k - 1$ positions.

Warnings

The translation of imperative languages is now complete. For didactical reasons, we have made several simplifications. Some important real-world complications have been ignored. One such complication is incurred by bounded word sizes.

Let us focus on the treatment of constants. We have liberally allowed arbitrary *int* constants as parts of CMA instructions, sometimes even two constant operands for one instruction. A machine similar to our C-Machine, but for PASCAL – the P-Machine – has differentiated between cases in which the constant operands fit within the admissible space for the instruction and those where this is not the case. Large constants were placed in a dedicated constant table. Such a table is also mandatory for arbitrary length constants such as strings. The instructions may contain references to this table. The same operation may be implemented by several instructions that differ in that they expect their operands in the instruction itself or in the constant table. In the latter case, relative addresses are stored in the instruction itself. The compiler, or a downstream assembler in the case of the Zürich P4 compiler, generated different instructions depending on the sizes of the constants and stored the constants in the instructions or the constant table.

Open Questions and Further References

In this chapter we have *specified* the translation of a C-like language into a language of a suitable virtual machine. By now, the interested reader might want to know how to *implement* the given translation schemes.

- The translation schemes are defined by recursion on the syntactic structure of programs. They assume that the syntactic structure is known. Given a suitable hierarchical representation of programs, the schemes can be combined to the definition of recursive code functions. One might wonder whether the same recursive functions could also recognize the structure of programs beforehand. To a certain extent this is possible, and we will discuss efficient methods for recognizing the structure of programs in the subsequent volume.
- For the compilation of assignments and expressions, the types of variables and expressions were used. We did not specify how the type of an expression is determined. That is part of the static analysis, which will also be discussed in the next volume.
- In the examples, we realized that the translation schemes did not always lead to the optimal, that is, the most efficient CMA instruction sequence. Techniques for improving translation schemes that lead to better, maybe even optimal, instruction sequences, will be addressed in Volume 4 on code generation. Here, non-local information about dynamic, that is run-time, properties is needed. Techniques for such static program analysis are discussed in depth in Volume 3.
- The use of virtual machines simplifies code generation. New problems arise if target programs for real machines are to be generated in a way that exploits the

potentials offered by their architectures. One problem is to optimally make use of the register file of the target machine. Such problems will also be addressed in Volume 4.

2.11 Exercises

1. *Code generation for expressions.*
   Generate CMA code for the following expressions:

   $$a \leftarrow 2 \cdot (c + (b - 3))$$
   $$b \leftarrow b \cdot (a + 3)$$

   Assume the following address environment:

   $$\rho = \{a \mapsto 5, b \mapsto 6, c \mapsto 7\}$$

   Execute the generated code by displaying the stack contents after each instruction! Assume that the variables are initialized with the values $a = 22$, $b = 33$ and $c = 44$.

2. *Code generation for loops.*
   Generate CMA code for the two loops:

   while $(x > y)$ {
       if $(2 \cdot y > x)$ $y \leftarrow y + x$;
       else $x \leftarrow x - y$;
   }

   for $(x \leftarrow 0; x < 42; x \leftarrow x + z)$
       if $(\neg(x = y))z \leftarrow z + 1$;

   Use the following address environment:

   $$\rho = \{x \mapsto 2, y \mapsto 3, z \mapsto 5\}$$

3. *Code generation for statement sequences.*
   Consider the following sequence of statements:

$$z \leftarrow 1;$$
$$\textbf{while } (n > 0) \{$$
$$\qquad j \leftarrow 1;$$
$$\qquad y \leftarrow x;$$
$$\qquad \textbf{while } (2 \cdot j \leq n) \{$$
$$\qquad\qquad y \leftarrow y \cdot y;$$
$$\qquad\qquad j \leftarrow j \cdot 2;$$
$$\qquad \}$$
$$\qquad z \leftarrow y \cdot z;$$
$$\qquad n \leftarrow n - j;$$
$$\}$$

- What does this statement sequence compute?
- Translate the statement sequence into CMA code! Use the following address environment:

$$\rho = \{n \mapsto 1, j \mapsto 2, x \mapsto 3, y \mapsto 4, z \mapsto 5\}$$

4. *Reverse engineering.*
   Consider the following CMA code:

loadc 0		**pop**		**storea** 1
loadc 1		**jump** B		**pop**
loadc 13	$A:$	**loada** 3		**loadc** 2
loada 3		**loada** 2		**loada** 2
loadc 1		**geq**		**mul**
le		**jumpz** B		**storea** 2
jumpz A		**loada** 1		**pop**
loadc -1		**loadc** 1		**jump** A
storea 1		**add**	$B:$	**halt**

- Execute this CMA code. Assume that prior to program execution the value of *SP* is 0.
- What does the given code compute when the memory location with address 3 is given as input?

5. *Short circuit evaluation.*
   Let b, e_1, and e_2 be arbitrary expressions:
   - A conditional expression in C has the form $b ? e_1 : e_2$. Its value is the value of e_1 if $b \neq 0$ and the value of e_2 if $b = 0$.
     Design a translation scheme for $\text{code}_R (b ? e_1 : e_2) \rho$.
   - *Short circuit evaluation* for a Boolean expression means that the second term of a conjunction (disjunction) is not evaluated if the evaluation of the first term is already 0 (or a non-zero value in the case of a disjunction).

Give translation schemes for $\text{code}_R \ (e_1 \wedge e_2) \ \rho$ (and $\text{code}_R \ (e_1 \vee e_2) \ \rho$) using *short circuit evaluation*!

6. *Breaks.*

   Modify the scheme for the translation of loops so that it can deal with *break* statements, which cause the immediate exit from the loop! For this, extend the translation function with a further argument l, which specifies the jump target to which control proceeds in the case of a **break**.

7. *Continues.*

   A **continue** statement causes a jump to the end of the body of the enclosing loop. How must the translation schemes be modified in order to correctly translate **continue** statements at arbitrary locations?

   Hint: Extend the translation function with yet another argument!

8. *Jump tables I.*

   Extend the translation scheme for the *switch* statement to allow negative values as cases and also (singular and small) gaps within the range of case values.

   Dream up heuristics to deal with large and irregular gaps.

9. *Jump tables II.*

   We have translated the *switch* statement by means of a relative jump into the jump table from which a further direct jump leads to the start address of the selected alternative. The first jump can be saved if the jump table does not contain jump instructions but jump targets. Then the instruction **jumpi** must be replaced by an instruction **jumpi'**, which jumps straight to the address stored in the table. There are two variants:

   a) The jump table is located *after* the code for individual cases. Then the **jumpi'** receives the start address of the table as argument;

   b) The jump table is located directly behind the instruction **jumpi'**, that is, *before* the code for the individual cases. Then, the start address must be provided as an argument to the instruction.

   Define adequate instructions **jumpi'** for both cases and give translation schemes for each!

10. *Code generation for pointers.*

    Consider the following definitions:

```
int * m, n;
struct list {
        int info;
        struct list * next;
        } * l, * tmp;
m ← malloc(sizeof(int));
*m ← 4;
l ← null;
for (n ← 5; n ≤ *m; n−−) {
        tmp ← l;
        l ← malloc(sizeof(struct list));
        l → next ← tmp;
        l → info ← n;
}
```

- Compute an address environment for the variables.
- Generate code for the program.
- Execute the generated code.

11. *Extreme Pointer.*
In order to set the Extreme Pointer EP, the compiler requires the maximal size of the local stack. This value can be computed at compile-time.

Define a function t that computes for the expression e a precise upper bound $t(e)$ for the number of stack locations that are maximally needed for the evaluation of e.
- Compute $t(e)$ for the two extreme cases:

$$a_1 + (a_2 + (\cdots + (a_{n-1} + a_n) \ldots)) \quad \text{and} \quad (\ldots ((a_1 + a_2) + a_3) + \ldots) + a_n$$

(a_i constants or basic type variables).
- Compute $t(e)$ for the expressions given in Exercise 1 and Example 2.8.1.
- Extend the definition of the function t to C statements, in particular, *if*, *for*, and *while* statements.

12. *Blocks.*
Extend the code generation function for statement sequences to blocks. For this, allow that variable declarations may occur in arbitrary positions within a block. Declared variables are supposed to be visible from the point where they are introduced to the end of the current block.
As an example, consider the following program:

$$\textbf{int } x;$$
$$x \leftarrow 1;$$
$$\{$$
$$\qquad \textbf{int } x;$$
$$\qquad x \leftarrow 2;$$
$$\qquad \text{write}(x);$$
$$\}$$
$$\text{write}(x);$$

Here, variable x first receives the value of 1. Another variable with the name x is introduced in the inner block, which receives the value 2. When the inner block is finished, this second variable x disappears and the first variable x with value of 1 becomes visible again.

Hint: Together with the address environment, maintain the first relative address behind the locals.

13. *Initialization of variables.*

Modify the function code so that variables can be initialized. For example, it should be possible to compile the following definition:

$$\textbf{int } a \leftarrow 0;$$

14. *Post- and preincrement.*   Give transation schemes for:
    - ++ and -- (prefix and postfix).
    - $+ \leftarrow$ and $- \leftarrow$.

Take care that the operators are not only defined for variables, but can also be applied to arbitrary expressions.

15. *Code generation for functions.*

Consider the following definitions:

```
int n;
struct tree {
    int info;
    struct tree * left, *right;
} * t;
struct tree * mktree (int d, int * n) {
    struct tree * t;
    if (d ≤ 0) return null;
    else {
        t ← malloc(sizeof(struct tree));
        t → left ← mktree(d − 1, n);
        t → info ← *n; *n ← *n + 1;
        t → right ← mktree(d − 1, n);
        return t;
    }
}
```

Compute the address environment for the function *mktree* and generate code for the function as well as for the assignment:

$$t \leftarrow mktree(5, \&n);$$

16. *Reference parameters.*

    C++ offers, in addition to parameter passing *by value*, also parameter passing *by reference*. Consider the following code fragment:

    ```
    int a;
    void f (int &x) { x ← 7; }
    int main() {
        f(a); return 0;
    }
    ```

    if the formal parameter x is used in the body of the function f, then the target variable is the one whose L-value has been passed to x as actual parameter. After the execution of $f(a)$, the variable a should contain the value 7.

    Translate the example program and check that it behaves as expected.

17. *Variable argument lists.*

    In this exercise, we consider functions with variable argument lists. The parameter lists of such functions first enumerate the mandatory parameters, followed by "..." for the optional ones. Given that these all have type t, the R-value of the next optional parameter should be accessed by means of the call $next(t)$. Consider for example the function:

```
int sum(int n, ...) {        //   Sum of n numbers
    int result ← 0;
    while (n > 0) {
        result ← result + next(int);
        n ← n − 1;
    }
    return result;
}
```

Possible calls are for example $sum\,(5, a, b, c, d, e)$ and $sum\,(3, 1, 2, 3)$.

- Verify whether our translation for such function calls is adequate.
- Invent an implementation for $next(t)$.

18. *Code generation for programs.*
    Translate the following program:

```
int result;
int fibo (int n) {
    int result;
    if (n < 0) return −1;
    switch (n) {
        case 0  : return 0; break;
        case 1  : return 1; break;
        default : return fibo (n − 1) + fibo (n − 2);
    }
}
int main() {
    int n;
    n ← 5;
    result ← fibo (n);
    return 0;
}
```

19. CMA *interpreters.*
    Implement an interpreter for the C-Machine in the programming language of your choice.

- Choose a suitable data type for instructions. Take into account that some instructions have arguments, but some have not.
- Implement the datastructures C and S.
- Test your interpreter with the factorial function and the main function:

$$\textbf{int } main() \; \{ \; \textbf{return } fac(9); \; \}$$

2.12 List of CMA Registers

EP, Extreme Pointer   p. 28
FP, Frame Pointer   p. 35
HP, Heap Pointer   p. 27
PC, Program Counter   p. 8
SP, Stack Pointer   p. 8

2.13 List of Code Functions of the CMA

code   p. 12
code$_L$ p. 12
code$_R$ p. 12

2.14 List of CMA Instructions

add	p. 10	**jumpz**	p. 16	**neg**	p. 11
and	p. 10	**jumpi**	p. 20	**neq**	p. 10
alloc	p. 42	**leq**	p. 10	**new**	p. 28
call	p. 40	**le**	p. 10	**or**	p. 10
div	p. 10	**load**	p. 13	**pop**	p. 15
dup	p. 21	**loada**	p. 14	**return**	p. 44
enter	p. 41	**loadc**	p. 9	**slide**	p. 42
eq	p. 10	**loadr**	p. 38	**store**	p. 13
geq	p. 10	**loadrc**	p. 37	**storea**	p. 14
gr	p. 10	**malloc**	p. 28	**storer**	p. 38
halt	p. 46	**mark**	p. 40	**sub**	p. 10
jump	p. 16	**mul**	p. 10		

2.15 References

Language-oriented virtual machines have been around for quite a while. They have been introduced for simplifying compilation and for porting to different machines. In [RR64] a virtual machine for ALGOL60, the *Algol Object Code* (AOC), was described.

The model for current virtual machines for imperative languages is the P-Machine which was used for the widely distributed P4 Pascal compiler from Zürich. It is described in [Amm81] and in [PD82], where sources for the P4 compiler, assembler, and P-Machine interpreter can be found.

3

Functional Programming Languages

3.1 Basic Concepts and Introductory Examples

Functional programming languages have their origin in LISP and, thus, can be traced back to as early as 1958. It is, however, only since the end of the Seventies that this class of languages has freed itself from the dominance of LISP and developed novel concepts and implementation techniques.

Imperative languages know (at least) two worlds: the world of expressions and the world of statements. Expressions generate values while statements change values of variables or modify the control flow. In imperative languages, the values of variables can be changed as a *side-effect* when evaluating statements. Functional languages, on the other hand, only know expressions. Accordingly, executing a functional program means evaluating a given *program expression* that describes the result value of the program. For its evaluation, further expressions may be evaluated, for example, when an expression consists of function applications. Control flow via specific statements does not exist. Variables in functional programs can be *bound* to expressions. Variables are, thus, not identifiers for memory locations whose value can be changed like in imperative languages. Executing the program, may only *evaluate* expressions that are bound to variables. Once evaluated, a variable is bound to a single value.

In the following, we explain the most important concepts of modern functional programming languages. For a concrete syntax, we use the programming language OCAML.

Function definitions. A function is obtained by *abstracting* variables from an expression. An expression

$$\textbf{fun } x\, y \to x + y$$

defines a function with formal parameters x, y and the defining expression $x + y$, which is supposed to produce the return value. The abstracted expression represents an *anonymous* function, that is a nameless function. In our example, the function can be applied to two arguments:

$$(\textbf{fun } x\, y \to x + y)\ 1\ 2$$

R. Wilhelm, H. Seidl, *Compiler Design*, DOI 10.1007/978-3-642-14909-2_3,
© Springer-Verlag Berlin Heidelberg 2010

It is often practical to introduce a name to a function defined via abstraction. This name can then be used to denote the function:

$$\textbf{let } add \ = \ \textbf{fun } x \, y \rightarrow x + y$$
$$\textbf{in } add \, 1 \, (add \, 2 \, 3)$$

Recursive Definitions. If the name of a function is used in its own defining expression, then the function is *recursive*. Technically, such a definition can be understood as a (functional) *recursion equation*. The definition

$$\textbf{let rec } log = \textbf{fun } x \rightarrow \textbf{if } x \leq 1 \textbf{ then } 0$$
$$\textbf{else } 1 + log \, (x/2)$$

binds the name *log* to the expression on the right side, which itself also refers to the name on the left side of the definition. In programming languages with lazy evaluation, non-functional values can be recursively defined as well, such as (potentially) infinite lists.

Pattern Matching. Functions on structured algebraic types such as lists can be defined through case distinction. The different cases are given by *patterns*, which are matched against values of that type. If the pattern matches a value, the variables that occur in the pattern are bound to the corresponding components of the value. In the expression:

$$\textbf{match } [1;2;3] \textbf{ with}$$
$$[1;x;y] \rightarrow x + y$$
$$\mid \quad [z] \rightarrow z$$

for instance, the first alternative is chosen. Then the variables x and y are bound to the components 2 and 3, and their sum is returned. This comparison against patterns is called *pattern matching*.

Higher-Order Functions. A function is of *higher-order* if it may take functions as arguments and/or return functions as results. To understand this concept, consider the function *map* from the standard library of OCAML. The function *map* receives as first argument a function f and as second argument a list l. The call *map f l* applies the function f to all elements in the list l and returns the list of the results:

$$\textbf{let rec } map = \textbf{fun } f \, l \rightarrow \textbf{match } l \textbf{ with}$$
$$[] \rightarrow []$$
$$\mid x :: xs \rightarrow f \, x :: map \, f \, xs$$

Depending on the value of the second parameter, the function differentiates two cases. If *map* is called with a function and an empty list, an empty list is returned. If the second argument is a non-empty list, there are two subsequent calls. First, the function f is called with the first element of the list. Then *map* is recursively called with f and the rest of the list. Both results then are combined to form the result list. The function *map* is a *higher-order* function, since it expects a function as an argument.

Let us note that besides the puristic syntax used so far, the programming language OCAML also allows us to list the formal parameters in a function definition following the function name:

$$\textbf{let rec } map \ f \ l = \textbf{ match } l \textbf{ with}$$
$$[] \to []$$
$$| \ x :: xs \to f \ x :: map \ f \ xs$$

Polymorphism. Types in functional programming languages are often represented as terms. Basic types are atomic terms, such as **int**, **bool**. Structured types, such as lists, are described by type terms. A list of **int** values is, for example, described by **int list**. An expression may have more than one possible type. In OCAML, the set of possible types of an expression can be described by a *type scheme*. A type scheme may contain *type variables*, which may be instantiated to different types at different uses of the expression. The type scheme for an expression can be specified by a declaration or be derived by a *type inference algorithm*. A type inference algorithm derives, for all expressions for which the programmer has not specified a type, a type scheme, which is as general as possible (often *the* most general) and then verifies that all expressions are used according to their types. The function *map*, for example, has the *polymorphic* type:

$$map : ('a \to 'b) \to 'a \textbf{ list} \to 'b \textbf{ list}$$

The type variables $'a, 'b$ stand for any types. This means that the function *map* can be used for an *int* function and an *int* list, as well as for a Boolean function and a list of Boolean values. The type of *map* only requires that the argument type of the first functional argument agrees with the type of the elements of the second argument, which is a list. The result then has a list type, where the list elements have the type of the result of the functional argument.

In the following sections, we present a simple functional fragment FUL of OCAML as well as the architecture of the virtual machine MAMA. Then we explain the instruction set of the MAMA together with the translation schemes for the translation of FULinto MAMA code. After a description of the architecture, the translation is explained for simple expressions first, as we did in Sect. 2.2. After the treatment of variables, we proceed in the same spirit as we proceeded for the translation of C into CMA code. Novel concepts, though, are needed for implementing lazy evaluation and higher-order functions.

3.2 A Simple Functional Programming Language

As in Chap. 2, we are interested in code generation for a well-suited virtual machine rather than in further tasks of compilation such as parsing or type checking. To simplify things, we consider a fragment of the programming language OCAML, which we call FUL (**Fu**nctional **L**anguage). In order to avoid awkward case distinctions, we allow **int** as the only basic type. That means that we assume, like with the programming language C, but in contrast to OCAML, that conditions return *int* values, which can be tested for zero (false) or non-zero (true). Later, we will extend our core language with composite data structures such as tuples and lists.

As programs, we consider expressions e of the form:

$$e ::= b \mid x \mid (\square_1\, e) \mid (e_1\, \square_2\, e_2)$$
$$\mid (\textbf{if } e_0 \textbf{ then } e_1 \textbf{ else } e_2)$$
$$\mid (e'\, e_0 \ldots e_{k-1}) \mid (\textbf{fun } x_0 \ldots x_{k-1} \rightarrow e)$$
$$\mid (\textbf{let } x = e \textbf{ in } e_0)$$
$$\mid (\textbf{let rec } x_1 = e_1 \textbf{ and } \ldots \textbf{ and } x_n = e_n \textbf{ in } e_0)$$

where $\square_1$ and $\square_2$ identify arbitrary unary and binary operators on *int* values. An expression is thus:

- a basic value, a variable, the application of an operator, or a conditional expression;
- a function application;
- a function resulting from an expression by abstracting its formal parameters;
- a *let* expression, which introduces a local definition, or
- a *letrec* expression, which introduces local (recursive) definitions.

Example 3.2.1 The following well-known function *fac* computes the factorial:

$$\textbf{let rec } \textit{fac} \quad = \quad \textbf{fun } x \ \rightarrow \quad \textbf{if } x \leq 1 \textbf{ then } 1$$
$$\textbf{else } x \cdot \textit{fac}\, (x - 1)$$
$$\textbf{in} \quad \textit{fac}\ 13$$

As usual, we only place brackets where they are required for understanding. In a sequence of expressions without brackets such as $e'\, e_0 \ldots e_{k-1}$ it is understood that e' represents the function and the expressions $e_0, \ldots, e_{k-1}$ are the actual parameters of the function. □

The semantics of function application still requires us to specify two aspects. The first concerns parameter passing, that is, *what* is passed to the function within a function application. The second concerns the interpretation of *free* variables. In the previous chapter, these were called *global variables*. For free variables, we can use *static* or *dynamic* scoping. With static scoping, the value of a free variable is determined by the *closest* textually enclosing scope, while with dynamic scoping, the value is determined by the chronologically *latest* binding.

The parameter passing mechanism of a programming language determines in which form actual parameters are passed. ALGOL60 and later PASCAL and C, offer parameter passing *by value*. ALGOL60 additionally offers parameter passing *by name*, and PASCAL, as well as C++, also offers parameter passing *by reference*. The latter mechanism is meaningless for functional languages, as these have no concept of reference. Parameters, therefore, can only be passed as values or as *expressions*.

The *evaluation order* determines whether in a function application $e' \, e_0 \ldots e_{k-1}$, the actual parameters $e_0, \ldots, e_{k-1}$ are evaluated or whether their evaluation is postponed. There are two choices. Either the actual parameters $e_0, \ldots, e_{k-1}$ are evaluated *before* evaluation proceeds to the evaluation of the expression e'. Alternatively, evaluation may directly proceed to the evaluation of the expression e'. Assume that this evaluation has returned a function **fun** $x_0 \ldots x_{m-1} \rightarrow e$ and that the number k of available arguments is sufficiently large, that is, $m \leq k$. Then evaluation further proceeds to the body e of the function. This means that the formal parameters x_i are bound to the unevaluated expressions e_i – while evaluation of the e_i is postponed, until their values are required for determining the value of e.

Example 3.2.2 Consider the functional program:

$$
\begin{aligned}
\textbf{let rec} \quad & fac \quad = \quad \ldots \\
\textbf{and} \quad & foo \quad = \quad \textbf{fun } x \, y \rightarrow x \\
\textbf{in } & foo \; 1 \; (fac \; 1000)
\end{aligned}
$$

where the function *fac* is the factorial function. The function *foo* is expected to return the value of its first parameter. The evaluation order makes a big difference in this case. If all actual parameters are evaluated first, a rather expensive computation is triggered to determine the value of the sub-expression $(fac \; 1000)$, which may even cause memory overflow with abnormal program termination. The second parameter, however, is not needed for determining the result value of the program! If the body of the function *foo* is evaluated first, evaluation terminates quickly with the value 1, and a possible memory overflow is avoided.   □

According to this discussion, we distinguish three cases:

Call-By-Value or *Applicative Order Evaluation*:

> The parameters are evaluated first and their values are passed to the function. This is the evaluation strategy of OCAML.
>
> *Advantage:* The parameters are evaluated only once; no extra overhead is incurred beyond the evaluation itself.
>
> *Disadvantage:* Some parameters are evaluated even though they may not be needed for the evaluation of the function body. This can be critical when the evaluation of the parameter is expensive, leads to a run-time error, or does not terminate.

Call-By-Name or *Normal Order Evaluation*:

> Evaluation starts with the function body. If the value of a parameter is needed, the corresponding expression is evaluated.
>
> *Advantage:* No parameter is evaluated whose value is not required. In our Example 3.2.2, evaluating the call $(fac \; 1000)$ is avoided. In general, *call-by-name* has a better termination behavior than *call-by-value*.
>
> *Disadvantage:* If the value of a parameter is needed multiple times, the corresponding expression is evaluated multiple times.

Call-By-Need or *Lazy Evaluation*:

> A parameter is only evaluated if its value is needed, and then just once. The first use, thus, forces us to evaluate the parameter. All subsequent uses may access the value, which has already been memorized. This strategy is used for example by the programming language HASKELL.

Call-by-need can be seen as an optimization of *call-by-name*, which tries to combine the good termination behavior of *call-by-name* with the efficiency of *call-by-value*. Postponing the evaluation of subexpressions is, however, not for free: it requires additional management overhead. For the programming language FUL, we leave the strategy for parameter passing open and present translation schemes both for *call-by-value* (*CBV*) and *call-by-need* (*CBN*).

For the discussion of parameter passing, we have so far left open whether static or dynamic scoping is used, even though these two considerations are not independent of each other. With *static scoping*, the use of a name always relates to the textually innermost enclosing construct that defines the name. With *dynamic scoping*, the dynamically last binding for a name defines the value of the name.

Example 3.2.3 Consider the following program:

$$
\begin{aligned}
&\textbf{let}\quad x = 2\ \textbf{in}\\
&\textbf{let}\quad f = \textbf{fun}\ y \to x + y\ \textbf{in}\\
&\textbf{let}\quad h = \textbf{fun}\ g\ x \to g\ 2\ \textbf{in}\\
&\qquad h\ f\ 1
\end{aligned}
$$

With static scoping, the free variable x in the body of f refers to the definition $x = 2$. Therefore, the value of $h\ f\ 1$ is 4. With dynamic scoping, x is bound to 1, before the value of x is accessed in the body of f. Consequently, the value is 3.   □

Evaluation with static scoping leads always to the same result, as expressions have a fixed binding for their free variables. This property is also called *referential transparency*. As with all modern functional programming languages, we choose static scoping for FUL.

This choice affects the implementation of function application. Consider again the application $h\ f\ 1$ with *call-by-need* parameter passing. Static scoping enforces that the free variable x in the definition **fun** $y \to x + y$ of f obtains its value according to the textually enclosing *let*-construct. In this particular example, x is therefore bound to the value 2.

Such a binding is also called an *environment*. In order to ensure that for each *free* variable in the expression e_i for a formal parameter x_i, always the correct environment is available at each use of e_i, the appropriate environment must be passed along with the expression e_i. Note that this environment is only known at run-time. The resulting pair of an expression and an environment for all free variables in the expression is called a *closure*. Sometimes, environments are also required for programs with *call-by-value* parameter passing. This is the case when, as in Example 3.2.3, functions may contain free variables.

Formally, the set of free variables, free(e), are defined by induction on the structure of the program expressions e as follows:

$$
\begin{aligned}
\text{free}(b) &= \emptyset & (b \text{ a basic value}) \\
\text{free}(x) &= \{x\} & (x \text{ a variable}) \\
\text{free}(\square_1 e) &= \text{free}(e) \\
\text{free}(e_1 \square_2 e_2) &= \text{free}(e_1) \cup \text{free}(e_2) \\
\text{free}(\mathbf{if}\ e_0\ \mathbf{then}\ e_1\ \mathbf{else}\ e_2) &= \text{free}(e_0) \cup \text{free}(e_1) \cup \text{free}(e_2) \\
\text{free}(e' e_0 \ldots e_{k-1}) &= \text{free}(e') \cup \text{free}(e_0) \cup \ldots \cup \text{free}(e_{k-1}) \\
\text{free}(\mathbf{fun}\ x_0 \ldots x_{k-1} \to e') &= \text{free}(e') \setminus \{x_0, \ldots, x_{k-1}\} \\
\text{free}(\mathbf{let}\ x = e_1\ \mathbf{in}\ e_0) &= \text{free}(e_1) \cup (\text{free}(e_0) \setminus \{x\}) \\
\text{free}(\mathbf{let\ rec}\ x_1 = e_1\ \mathbf{and}\ \ldots\ \mathbf{and}\ x_n = e_n\ \mathbf{in}\ e_0) & \\
&= (\text{free}(e_0) \cup \ldots \cup \text{free}(e_n)) \setminus \{x_1, \ldots, x_n\}
\end{aligned}
$$

Example 3.2.4 The set of free variables of the expression:

$$\mathbf{if}\ x \leq 1\ \mathbf{then}\ 1\ \mathbf{else}\ x \cdot fac\ (x - 1)$$

is $\{x, fac\}$. If we abstract the variable x in this expression, that is, we place $\mathbf{fun}\ x \to$ before the expression, the variable x is *bound*. Then *fac* is the only remaining free variable. □

3.3 The Architecture of the MAMA

In the following, we outline the architecture of a virtual machine for FUL. The machine is called MAMA, after its creator Dieter Maurer (**Ma**urer **Ma**chine). Its design closely follows the C-Machine, our virtual machine for imperative languages. MAMA, like the C-Machine, provides a program store C where MAMA programs are stored. Each memory location may contain a virtual instruction. The register PC (Program Counter) contains the address of the instruction to be executed next. The main execution cycle for executing virtual machine programs is the same as that for the C-Machine:

- Load the next instruction.
- Increment PC by 1.
- Execute the loaded instruction.

Like the C-Machine, The MAMA has an instruction **halt**, which terminates program execution and returns control to the operating system.

The run-time stack S with the registers SP and FP has also already been introduced for the C-Machine. Each memory location in S is large enough to contain a basic value or an address. The register SP always points to the topmost occupied location in S. With respect to the total space available for program execution, we are slightly more generous for the MAMA than we were for the C-Machine: we assume that there is always enough space for the stack.

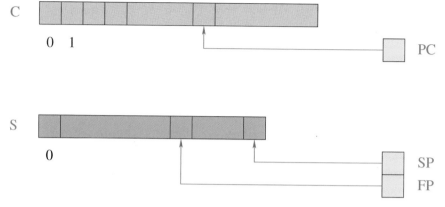

Fig. 3.1. The architecture of the MAMA

In contrast to the C-Machine, values in the MAMA are always created in the heap H (Fig. 3.2). The heap H can be seen as an *abstract data type*, which provides an operation

$$new\ T\,(args)$$

which creates a new MAMA-object in the heap H with label T and arguments *args* and returns a reference to the object on top of the stack S.

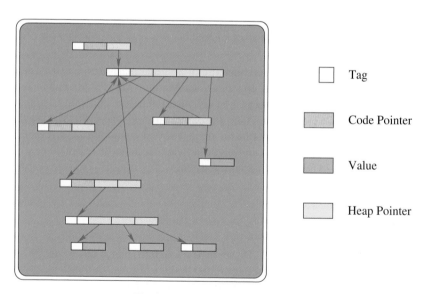

Fig. 3.2. The heap of the MAMA

Figure 3.3 lists the types of objects to be stored in the heap. Each of these objects

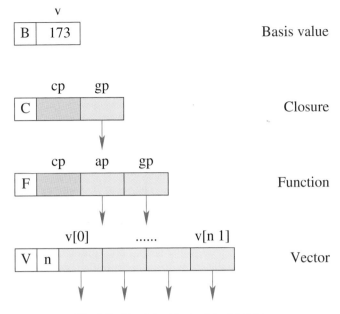

Fig. 3.3. The data objects of the MaMa

consists of a tag and, possibly, multiple data areas. A *B*-object represents a basic value. It consists of the tag *B* followed by an *int* value. References to multiple values can be aggregated into a *V*-object. In addition to the tag *V* and a specification of the length *n*, such an object contains a vector *v* with *n* entries. *C*- and *F*-objects represent closures and functional values, respectively. In addition to their respective tags, they contain a reference *cp* (Code Pointer) to an associated code section, as well as a reference *gp* (Global Pointer) to a *V* object representing the environment for free variables. Additionally, *F*-objects provide a reference *ap* (Argument Pointer) to a *V* object, which collects all arguments for the function that have already been provided.

Before we present the translation schemes for generating MaMa code for expressions, we must clarify what the generated sequence of instructions is supposed to produce as a result. According to our convention, values are stored in the heap. Thus, the translation function code$_V$ for an expression *e* is expected to compute the value of *e* and return a reference to the value on the stack.

With lazy evaluation, we need a different instruction sequence. This sequence is not supposed to evaluate *e*, but instead to construct a closure for *e*. In other words, it is supposed to construct a *C*-object for *e* in the heap and return a reference to this object on the stack. This is realized by the translation function code$_C$ which we will detail in Sect. 3.11. We first present the translation schemes of code$_V$.

3.4 Translation of Simple Expressions

We begin with the translation of *simple expressions*, which only consist of basic values, operators, and conditions. An example of such an expression is:

$$\textbf{if } a \leq b + 1 \textbf{ then } b - a \textbf{ else } a - b$$

As with the translation of C, code generation for the MAMA requires, in addition to the program fragment to be translated, an address environment ρ, which provides access to the bindings of free variables in the program fragment. We also remark that the arithmetic instructions such as **add** or **sub**, expect their arguments on top of the stack — and not references to values. The same also applies for comparisons and conditional jumps. Moreover, all results produced by these instructions are returned on the stack and not in the heap. For composite expressions it therefore seems quite inefficient to create the values of arguments to operators on the stack, then subsequently wrap them into B-objects in the heap, only to immediately unwrap them again to supply their content on the stack. As an optimization, we therefore introduce the translation function code_B, which translates an expression e into an instruction sequence that leaves the value of e on top of the stack. This function is analogous to the translation function code_R for computing R-values of expressions in C:

$$
\begin{aligned}
\text{code}_B \, b \, \rho \, sl \quad &= \quad \textbf{loadc } b \\[4pt]
\text{code}_B \, (\square_1 \, e) \, \rho \, sl \quad &= \quad \text{code}_B \, e \, \rho \, sl \\
&\quad\ \ \, \textbf{op}_1 \\[4pt]
\text{code}_B \, (e_1 \, \square_2 \, e_2) \, \rho \, sl \quad &= \quad \text{code}_B \, e_1 \, \rho \, sl \\
&\quad\ \ \, \text{code}_B \, e_2 \, \rho \, (sl + 1) \\
&\quad\ \ \, \textbf{op}_2 \\[4pt]
\text{code}_B \, (\textbf{if } e_0 \textbf{ then } e_1 \textbf{ else } e_2) \, \rho \, sl \quad &= \quad \text{code}_B \, e_0 \, \rho \, sl \\
&\quad\ \ \, \textbf{jumpz } A \\
&\quad\ \ \, \text{code}_B \, e_1 \, \rho \, sl \\
&\quad\ \ \, \textbf{jump } B \\
&\quad\ \ \, A : \text{code}_B \, e_2 \, \rho \, sl \\
&\quad\ \ \, B : ...
\end{aligned}
$$

$\textbf{op}_1$ and $\textbf{op}_2$ identify the instructions that implement the operators $\square_1$ and $\square_2$, respectively. Different from the translation function code_R, the translation function code_B requires, in addition to the address environment, a further argument, the current *stack level sl*. The stack level is meant to record the height of the local stack. This additional information will later be required for recovering the addresses of local variables.

For all other expressions, their values are first computed in the heap and, then, unwrapped to return them on top of the stack:

$$\text{code}_B\, e\, \rho\, sl = \text{code}_V\, e\, \rho\, sl$$
$$\textbf{getbasic}$$

where the instruction **getbasic** replaces the reference on top of the stack with the contents of the B-object to which it points (Fig. 3.4). If the reference does not point to a B-object, an error is reported. The analogous scheme for the translation of simple

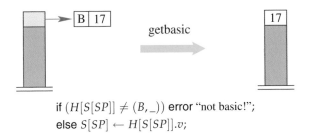

if $(H[S[SP]] \neq (B, \_))$ error "not basic!";
else $S[SP] \leftarrow H[S[SP]].v;$

Fig. 3.4. The instruction **getbasic**

expressions into V-Code is:

$$
\begin{array}{lcl}
\text{code}_V\, b\, \rho\, sl & = & \textbf{loadc } b;\ \textbf{mkbasic} \\[4pt]
\text{code}_V\, (\square_1\, e)\, \rho\, sl & = & \text{code}_B\, e\, \rho\, sl \\
 & & \textbf{op}_1;\ \textbf{mkbasic} \\[4pt]
\text{code}_V\, (e_1\, \square_2\, e_2)\, \rho\, sl & = & \text{code}_B\, e_1\, \rho\, sl \\
 & & \text{code}_B\, e_2\, \rho\, (sl + 1) \\
 & & \textbf{op}_2;\ \textbf{mkbasic} \\[4pt]
\text{code}_V\, (\textbf{if } e_0\, \textbf{then } e_1\, \textbf{else } e_2)\, \rho\, sl = & & \text{code}_B\, e_0\, \rho\, sl \\
 & & \textbf{jumpz } A \\
 & & \text{code}_V\, e_1\, \rho\, sl \\
 & & \textbf{jump } B \\
 & & A:\ \text{code}_V\, e_2\, \rho\, sl \\
 & & B:\ ...
\end{array}
$$

The idea is to switch to evaluation on the stack whenever possible, that is, to use B-Code whenever possible and to wrap the result of the evaluation into a B-object in the heap only at the very end. For this wrapping, we introduce the instruction **mkbasic** (Fig. 3.5). This instruction creates a new B-object for the value found on top of the stack:

Now we can already translate expressions such as:

$$2 + (\textbf{if } 3 \textbf{ then } 4 - 5 \textbf{ else } 0)$$

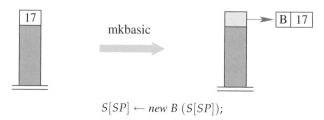

$$S[SP] \leftarrow new\ B\ (S[SP]);$$

Fig. 3.5. The instruction **mkbasic**

Expressions without variables are not very interesting. The key problem of accessing variables is addressed in the next section.

3.5 Access to Variables

Consider, for example, the function f:

$$\textbf{fun}\ a\ \rightarrow \textbf{let}\ b = a \cdot a$$
$$\textbf{in}\ b + c$$

The function f uses the *global* variable c and the *local* variables a (as a formal parameter) and b (introduced by **let**). According to the concept of static scoping, the value of a global variable has already been computed when the function is called and only needs to be looked up.

Therefore, the code generated by our translation aggregates the bindings of global variables into a V-object in the heap, the *global vector*. When constructing an F-object, the global vector for the function must be aggregated and a reference to it placed in the gp component. When evaluating an expression, the novel register GP (the Global Pointer) points to the current global vector. In contrast, local variables are maintained on the stack. In order to distinguish between local and global variables, the address environment has the form:

$$\rho : Vars \rightarrow \{L, G\} \times \mathbb{Z}$$

The global variables are enumerated consecutively and addressed *relative* to the start of the current global vector. The addressing of local variables, instead, crucially depends on the organization of the stack frames for function applications. In principle, there are two options.

Let $e'\ e_0\ \ldots\ e_{m-1}$ be the application of a function e' with arguments $e_0, \ldots, e_{m-1}$. The first option is to evaluate the actual parameters e_i from left to right and to push them onto the stack in this order (Fig. 3.6). If the register FP points to the top of the stack just before the evaluation of the arguments, these can be addressed relative to the FP. If the evaluation of the function e' happens to return a function f that has

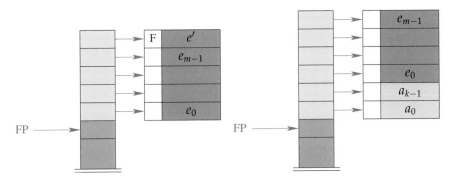

Fig. 3.6. A possible organization of the stack

already been applied to arguments $a_0, \ldots, a_{k-1}$, then these new parameters must be inserted, with some effort, beneath the other arguments into the stack.

Alternatively, a strategy could be chosen that has already been applied for the compilation of C function calls: the arguments are not evaluated from left to right, but from right to left (Fig. 3.7). In the case of C, this strategy proved to be useful because a C function may be called with further optional arguments. Let us now

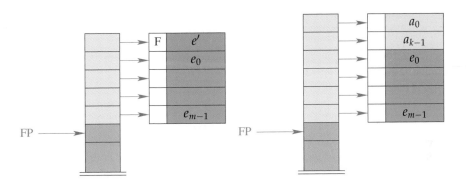

Fig. 3.7. A better organization of the stack

assume this order of arguments. If the FUL expression e' is evaluated to a function f that is partially applied to arguments $a_0, \ldots, a_{k-1}$, then these can be pushed directly on top of the stack.

This design choice has only one drawback: the formal parameters can now only be addressed relative to a fixed register if an additional auxiliary register is introduced (see Exercise 8). Instead of following this approach, we prefer to address local variables relative to the stack pointer SP.

This is not as unreasonable as it might seem. Although the register SP changes continuously during program execution, it points at each program point to an address on the stack that has a fixed distance to SP_0, the state the SP had at the last entrance of the enclosing function (Fig. 3.8). Moreover, this fixed distance $sl = SP - SP_0$ can be computed at translation time. It is the *stack level*, which we have used as an additional parameter to our code generation functions.

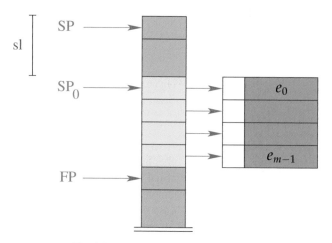

Fig. 3.8. The stack level of the MAMA

To the formal parameters $x_0, x_1, x_2, \ldots$ we consecutively assign the non-positive relative addresses $0, -1, -2, \ldots$, that is, $\rho\, x_i = (L, -i)$.

The *absolute* address of the i-th formal parameter is given by:

$$SP_0 + (-i) = (SP - sl) - i = SP - (sl + i)$$

The local variables $y_1, y_2, y_3, \ldots$ introduced via **let** or **let rec** constructs, are consecutively pushed on top of the stack (Fig. 3.9). Thus, the variables y_i receive positive relative addresses $1, 2, 3, \ldots$, that is, $\rho\, y_j = (L, j)$. The absolute address of the local variable y_j is given by:

$$SP_0 + j = (SP - sl) + j = SP - (sl - j)$$

In the case of *CBN*, we translate a variable access as follows:

$$\text{code}_\text{V}\ x\ \rho\ sl = \text{getvar}\ x\ \rho\ sl$$
$$\text{eval}$$

The instruction **eval** checks whether the value has been already computed or whether it still needs to be evaluated. This instruction is explained later. In the case of *CBV*, no closures are constructed. Since we can assume that the required values are available, the instruction **eval** is not necessary.

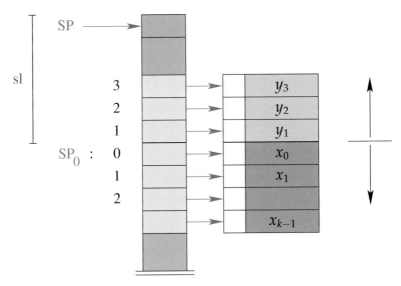

Fig. 3.9. The local variables of the MAMA

The macro getvar selects the actual instruction for the variable access, depending on the current address environment and the level of the stack. The macro getvar is defined by:

$$\text{getvar } x \, \rho \, sl = \textbf{match } \rho \, x \textbf{ with}$$
$$(L, i) \rightarrow \textbf{pushloc } (sl - i)$$
$$| \ (G, j) \rightarrow \textbf{pushglob } j$$

New instructions are required for handling local and global variables. To access a local variable, the instruction **pushloc** n is used (Fig. 3.10). This instruction pushes the contents of the stack location with address n relative to the current SP on top of the stack. Let sp and sl be the current value of the stack pointer SP and the stack

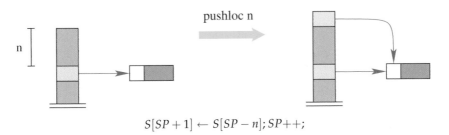

pushloc n

$$S[SP + 1] \leftarrow S[SP - n]; SP++;$$

Fig. 3.10. The instruction **pushloc** n

level, respectively. Our fixed reference point in the stack is given by $SP_0 = sp - sl$. The instruction **pushloc** $(sl - i)$ therefore is guaranteed to load the contents of the stack location with address:

$$sp - (sl - i) = (sp - sl) + i = sp_0 + i$$

Access to global variables is much easier. For this, the instruction **pushglob** j is introduced (Fig. 3.11). This instruction extracts the entry with index j from the vector to which register GP points, and pushes the entry onto the stack.

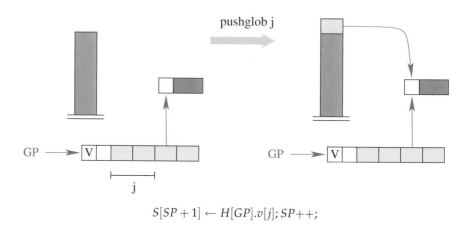

$$S[SP + 1] \leftarrow H[GP].v[j]; SP++;$$

Fig. 3.11. The instruction **pushglob** j

Example 3.5.1 Consider the expression $e \equiv (b + c)$ for the address environment $\rho = \{b \mapsto (L, 1), c \mapsto (G, 0)\}$ and a stack level $sl = 1$. Then, we obtain for *CBN*:

code$_V$ e ρ 1	= getvar b ρ 1	= 1 **pushloc** 0
	eval	2 eval
	getbasic	2 getbasic
	getvar c ρ 2	2 **pushglob** 0
	eval	3 eval
	getbasic	3 getbasic
	add	3 add
	mkbasic	2 mkbasic

In the first column we have generated all instructions for the expression, except those for accessing variables. These are determined in the second column using the respective stack levels before each instruction. These stack levels are displayed to the left of each instruction. The argument of the instruction **pushloc** therefore is determined as:

$$sl - \rho b = 1 - 1 = 0$$

☐

3.6 *let* **Expressions**

Consider local variables introduced by a *let* construct. Let $e \equiv$ **let** $x = e_1$ **in** e_0 be a
let expression. The translation of e must generate an instruction sequence that pushes
a new local variable x onto the stack. In the case of *CBV*, the expression e_1 must be
evaluated and x be bound to its value. In the case of *CBN*, evaluating the expression
e_1 is postponed until its value is actually required. Instead of computing the value of
e_1, a closure must be constructed for e_1, and a reference to it is recorded in x. Finally,
the expression e_0 must be evaluated and its value returned.

In the case of *CBN*, we therefore generate:

$$\text{code}_V \ e \ \rho \ sl = \text{code}_C \ e_1 \ \rho \ sl$$
$$\text{code}_V \ e_0 \ (\rho \oplus \{x \mapsto (L, sl+1)\}) \ (sl+1)$$
$$\textbf{slide 1}$$

The instruction *slide* releases the space for the local variable x. In the case of *CBV*,
the value of the variable x must be computed immediately. In this case, the expression
e_1 is translated by means of the code function code_V, instead by means of code_C.

Example 3.6.1 Consider the following expression:

$$e \equiv \textbf{let } a = 19 \textbf{ in let } b = a \cdot a \textbf{ in } a + b$$

for $\rho = \emptyset$ and $sl = 0$. In case of *CBV*, it is tranlated into:

0	**loadc 19**	3	**getbasic**	3	**pushloc 1**
1	**mkbasic**	3	**mul**	4	**getbasic**
1	**pushloc 0**	2	**mkbasic**	4	**add**
2	**getbasic**	2	**pushloc 1**	3	**mkbasic**
2	**pushloc 1**	3	**getbasic**	3	**slide 1**
				2	**slide 1**

☐

The instruction **slide** k releases the space of k local variables (Fig. 3.12). This more
general MAMA instruction suggests that it is impractical to free the space of each
local variable in a nested sequence of *let* instructions, as in Example 3.6.1. Instead, a
sequence of k **slide** 1 instructions should always be condensed into a single instruction **slide** k.

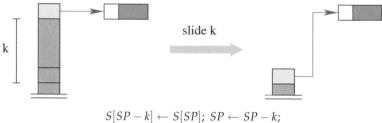

$$S[SP - k] \leftarrow S[SP];\ SP \leftarrow SP - k;$$

Fig. 3.12. The instruction **slide** k

3.7 Function Definitions

Let us now turn to the implementation of a function:

$$f \equiv \textbf{fun } x_0 \ldots x_{k-1} \to e$$

For the function f, code must be generated that constructs a *functional value* for f in the heap. This requires code for:

- creating a global vector for the free variables of f;
- creating an F-object that consists of an (initially empty) argument vector as well as the start address of the code for the evaluation of the body of the function; and finally,
- evaluating the body.

We convert these tasks directly into a translation scheme:

$$
\begin{aligned}
\mathrm{code}_V\,(\textbf{fun } x_0 \ldots x_{k-1} \to e)\,\rho\,sl = \quad & \textsf{getvar } z_0\ \rho\ sl \\
& \textsf{getvar } z_1\ \rho\ (sl+1) \\
& \quad \ldots \\
& \textsf{getvar } z_{g-1}\ \rho\ (sl+g-1) \\
& \textbf{mkvec } g \\
& \textbf{mkfunval } A \\
& \textbf{jump } B \\
A :\ & \textbf{targ } k \\
& \mathrm{code}_V\, e\, \rho'\, 0 \\
& \textbf{return } k \\
B :\ & \ldots
\end{aligned}
$$

where

$$
\begin{aligned}
\{z_0, \ldots, z_{g-1}\} &= \mathsf{free}(\textbf{fun } x_0 \ldots x_{k-1} \to e) \qquad \text{and} \\
\rho' &= \{x_i \mapsto (L, -i) \mid i = 0, \ldots, k-1\}\ \cup \\
& \quad\ \{z_j \mapsto (G, j) \mid j = 0, \ldots, g-1\}
\end{aligned}
$$

Note that the set of global variables is statically known: it can be determined by means of the function free. The sequence of calls to the macro getvar pushes the references to the global variables of the function successively onto the stack. For each further reference, the stack level is increased accordingly. The instruction **mkvec** g (Fig. 3.13) creates a vector in the heap that consists of the sequence of references to global variables from the top of the stack. It removes the corresponding references from the stack and pushes a reference to the newly constructed V-object onto the stack. The instruction **mkfunval** A (Fig. 3.14) constructs the F-object for a function

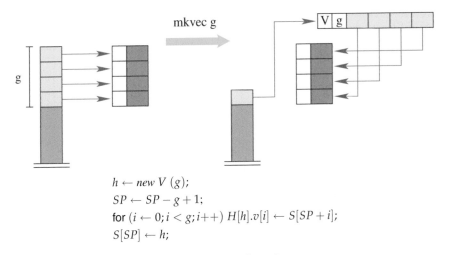

$$h \leftarrow new \ V \ (g);$$
$$SP \leftarrow SP - g + 1;$$
$$\text{for } (i \leftarrow 0; i < g; i++) \ H[h].v[i] \leftarrow S[SP + i];$$
$$S[SP] \leftarrow h;$$

Fig. 3.13. The instruction **mkvec** g

where A is the start address of the code, and the global vector is taken from the stack. Additionally, this instruction initializes the argument vector of the new F-object with an empty vector.

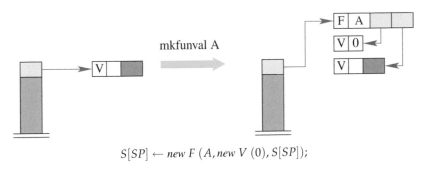

$$S[SP] \leftarrow new \ F \ (A, new \ V \ (0), S[SP]);$$

Fig. 3.14. The instruction **mkfunval** A

Our translation scheme also generates the code executed when an application of the function is to be evaluated. This is sensible as this code must use the same assignment of global variables to positions in the global vector that was used when including the variable bindings. On the other hand, this instruction sequence must not be executed when constructing the F-object itself: this code section therefore is skipped to continue at the location B.

The code for evaluating a function call, thus, is between the labels A and B. Essentially, it consists of the V-code for the body decorated with an instruction **targ** k at the beginning and an instruction **return** k at the end where k is the number of arguments of the function. These two instructions are discussed in Sect. 3.9. Here we just mention that the instruction **targ** k is responsible for undersupply with arguments, whereas the instruction **return** k is responsible for finalizing the evaluation of the call and a possible oversupply with arguments.

Example 3.7.1 Consider the function $f \equiv$ **fun** $b \rightarrow a + b$ for an address environment $\rho = \{a \mapsto (L, 1)\}$ and stack level $sl = 1$. The call $\text{code}_V\ f\ \rho\ 1$ is translated into:

1	**pushloc** 0	0	**pushglob** 0	2	**getbasic**
2	**mkvec** 1	1	**eval**	2	**add**
2	**mkfunval** A	1	**getbasic**	1	**mkbasic**
2	**jump** B	1	**pushloc** 1	1	**return** 1
0	A : **targ** 1	2	**eval**	2	B : ...

□

3.8 Function Application

Function applications are analogous to function calls in C. The instruction sequence generated for a function application must ensure that the state of the stack satisfies the assumptions of the code for the function definition when the function is entered. The necessary actions for evaluating a function application $e'\ e_0\ \ldots\ e_{m-1}$ are:

- allocating a stack frame;
- passing of parameters, that is, evaluating the actual parameters in the case of *CBV* or constructing closures for the actual parameters in the case of *CBN*;
- evaluating the function e' to an F-object;
- applying this function.

For *CBN*, this leads to the following translation scheme:

$$\text{code}_V \, (e' \, e_0 \, \ldots \, e_{m-1}) \, \rho \, sl = \quad \textbf{mark } A$$

$$\text{code}_C \, e_{m-1} \, \rho \, (sl+3)$$
$$\text{code}_C \, e_{m-2} \, \rho \, (sl+4)$$

$$\ldots$$

$$\text{code}_C \, e_0 \, \rho \, (sl+m+2)$$
$$\text{code}_V \, e' \, \rho \, (sl+m+3)$$
$$\textbf{apply}$$
$$A : \ldots$$

This scheme corresponds to the translation scheme for calls of C functions. The instruction **mark** A sets up a stack frame for the application. The actual parameters are evaluated from right to left. In the case of *CBN* semantics, code for constructing the required closures is generated. For this reason, code_C is used for the actual parameters e_i. In the case of *CBV* semantics, code is generated for evaluating the arguments, that is, code_V instead of code_C is used for the e_i. Note that with each reference pushed onto the stack, the stack level for the next call of the code generation function is increased.

After the actual parameters are translated, code is generated for determining the applied function. This happens by applying the code generation function code_V to e'. At run-time, the generated instruction sequence will push a reference to an F-object onto the stack. A further instruction therefore is needed to unpack this F-object and start the code for executing the function. This is realized by the instruction **apply**.

Example 3.8.1 For a call $(f \, 42)$ in the address environment $\rho = \{f \mapsto (L, 2)\}$ with a stack level $sl = 2$ our scheme generates for *CBV*:

2 **mark** A	6 **mkbasic**	7 **apply**
5 **loadc** 42	6 **pushloc** 4	3 $A : \ldots$

As a slightly larger example, consider the expression:

$$\textbf{let } a = 17 \textbf{ in let } f = \textbf{fun } b \rightarrow a + b \textbf{ in } f \, 42$$

We have already dealt with parts of this expression in previous examples. With *CBV* semantics, we obtain for sl = 0 altogether:

0	**loadc** 17	2	**jump** B	2	**getbasic**	5	**loadc** 42
1	**mkbasic**	0 $A:$	**targ** 1	2	**add**	5	**mkbasic**
1	**pushloc** 0	0	**pushglob** 0	1	**mkbasic**	6	**pushloc** 4
2	**mkvec** 1	1	**getbasic**	1	**return** 1	7	**apply**
2	**mkfunval** A	1	**pushloc** 1	2 $B:$	**mark** C	3 $C:$	**slide** 2
	□						

Before we describe the implementation of the new instructions, we must clarify how stack frames for evaluating a function call should be organized (Fig. 3.15). Like

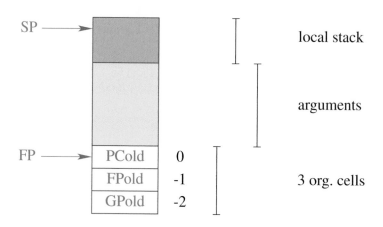

Fig. 3.15. The stack frame of the MaMa

the C-Machine, the MaMa requires three organizational cells, in which the values of the registers GP, FP, and PC are saved before the call, so that their values can be restored after the call. We fix that the frame pointer FP points to the topmost organizational cell. The arguments of the function are, thus, placed above the FP. The local stack for intermediate results and further local variables is placed above the arguments.

Now we are able to implement the instruction **mark** A (Fig. 3.16). In contrast

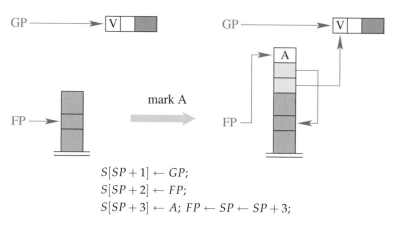

$$S[SP + 1] \leftarrow GP;$$
$$S[SP + 2] \leftarrow FP;$$
$$S[SP + 3] \leftarrow A; \ FP \leftarrow SP \leftarrow SP + 3;$$

Fig. 3.16. The instruction **mark** A

to the corresponding instruction of the C-Machine, this instruction saves all three registers. As with the C-Machine, the return address is pushed onto the stack at the

very end. For this reason, it requires as an argument the address to which program
execution is supposed to resume after the return from the function call. Further, it
sets the new Frame Pointer to the topmost organizational cell, here the saved PC.

The instruction **apply** must unpack the F-object to which (hopefully) a reference
is found on top of the stack, and must continue at the address cp provided by the F-
object (Fig. 3.17). We remark that the 0-th element of the argument vector is pushed

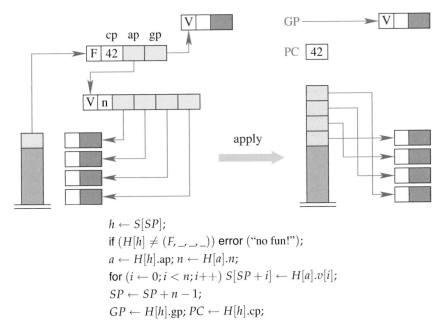

$$h \leftarrow S[SP];$$
$$\text{if } (H[h] \neq (F, \_, \_, \_)) \text{ error (``no fun!'');}$$
$$a \leftarrow H[h].\text{ap}; n \leftarrow H[a].n;$$
$$\text{for } (i \leftarrow 0; i < n; i++) \ S[SP + i] \leftarrow H[a].v[i];$$
$$SP \leftarrow SP + n - 1;$$
$$GP \leftarrow H[h].\text{gp}; PC \leftarrow H[h].\text{cp};$$

Fig. 3.17. The instruction **apply**

onto the stack first. This convention must be observed when constructing an F-object
for a function with an undersupply of arguments. This 0-th element of the vector thus
represents the *outermost* argument reference of such a function.

From the whole task of implementing functions, we now have dealt with the
following subtasks: generating F-objects from function definitions and, embedded
within, translating the function body in the correct environment; setting up a stack
frame for the function application and subsequently pushing of references to the arguments onto the stack; and, finally, starting the code for the function. What remains
is the decoration around the translation of the function body, namely, the instructions
targ k and **return** k. These are dealt with in the next section.

3.9 Under- and Oversupply with Arguments

The first instruction to be executed at run-time after an **apply** is the instruction **targ** k. This instruction checks whether enough arguments have been provided to execute the function body. The number of arguments is given by the difference $SP - FP$. If enough arguments are available, that is if $SP - FP \geq k$, then the function body is entered normally. If not enough arguments are available, that is if $SP - FP < k$, then **targ** k returns a new F-object as a result.

The instruction **targ** k is fairly complex. To better understand its effect, we divide its execution into several steps:

$$\textbf{targ } k = \textsf{if } (SP - FP < k) \; \{$$

$$\quad \textbf{mkvec0}; \qquad\qquad // \text{ creating the argument vector}$$

$$\quad \textbf{wrap}; \qquad\qquad\quad // \text{ creating the } F\text{-object}$$

$$\quad \textbf{popenv}; \qquad\qquad // \text{ releasing the stack frame}$$

$$\}$$

Aggregating this fixed sequence of tasks into a single instruction, once again, can be considered as an optimization.

In the case of undersupply with arguments, the first subtask is to aggregate the

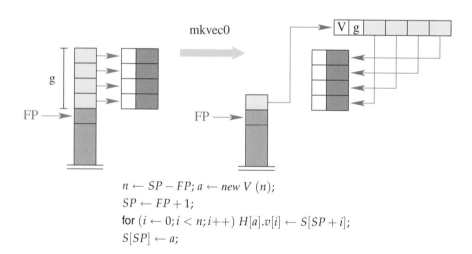

$$n \leftarrow SP - FP; \; a \leftarrow new \; V \; (n);$$
$$SP \leftarrow FP + 1;$$
$$\textsf{for } (i \leftarrow 0; i < n; i{+}{+}) \; H[a].v[i] \leftarrow S[SP + i];$$
$$S[SP] \leftarrow a;$$

Fig. 3.18. The instruction **mkvec0**

argument references between SP and FP into a vector. This is done by our microinstruction **mkvec0** (Fig. 3.18).

Subsequently, this argument vector is recorded in an F-object together with the current GP. This is implemented by the microinstruction **wrap** (Fig. 3.19). This instruction also records the start address of the code for executing the function call,

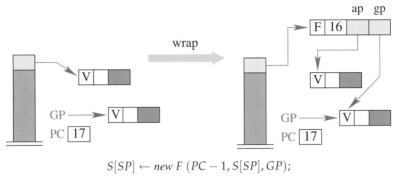

$$S[SP] \leftarrow new\ F\ (PC - 1, S[SP], GP);$$

Fig. 3.19. The instruction **wrap**

which is given by the address of the instruction **targ** k itself. As the PC does not change during the sequence of microinstructions, this address can be determined as the current content of the register PC minus 1.

Finally, it remains to release the stack frame and to return the created F-object as the result. This is realized by the microinstruction **popenv** (Fig. 3.20). Note that our

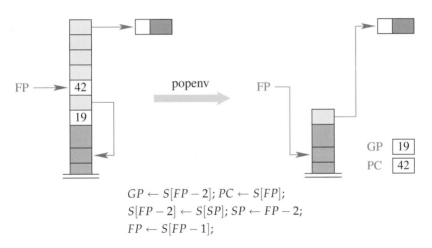

$$GP \leftarrow S[FP - 2];\ PC \leftarrow S[FP];$$
$$S[FP - 2] \leftarrow S[SP];\ SP \leftarrow FP - 2;$$
$$FP \leftarrow S[FP - 1];$$

Fig. 3.20. The instruction **popenv**

microinstruction **popenv** is more general than what is required for its use in **targ** k: an arbitrary number of further locations is allowed between the return value at the top of the stack and the organizational cells. In the case of undersupply with arguments we obtain for **targ** k the transformation in Fig. 3.21.

The instruction **return** k is responsible for finalizing the evaluation of function applications. Its argument k specifies the number of arguments consumed by the cur-

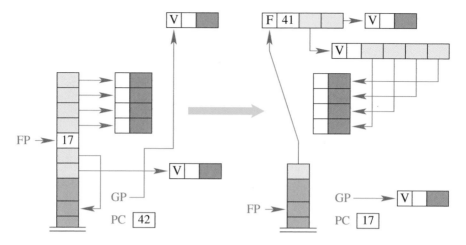

Fig. 3.21. The instruction **targ** k with undersupply with arguments

rent evaluation. It deals with two cases. If the stack frame contains exactly as many references to arguments as required by the called function, then the current stack frame is released and the result is returned. If, in constrast, the stack frame contains more references to arguments than required by the function, then an *oversupply* with arguments is detected. In this case, the current call should have produced a functional result value, which is able to consume further arguments. Because the result of the previous function evaluation has been provided at the top of the stack, above the arguments, the total number of arguments is given by $SP - FP - 1$. Again, the complex instruction **return** k is implemented by means of suitable microinstructions:

$$\textbf{return } k = \textbf{if } (SP - FP - 1 \le k)$$

popenv;	// release of the stack frame
else {	// further arguments exist
slide k;	
apply;	// repeated call
}	

Here, (micro-) instructions suffice that we have already introduced. The behavior of **return** k when the right number of arguments is provided is shown in Fig. 3.22. In this case the work is done by the microinstruction **popenv**.

The case when further, unconsumed arguments are found at the top of the stack is more complex. Then the instruction **slide** k removes the top k argument references since these are no longer needed. The instruction **apply** then triggers the evaluation of the F-object at the top of the stack. The overall effect of this case of oversupply is shown in Fig. 3.23. Note that the call triggered by the microinstruction **apply** reuses the stack frame of its predecessor.

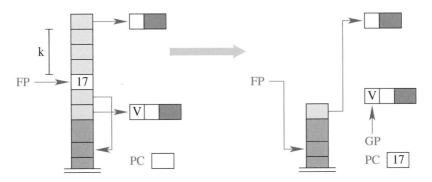

Fig. 3.22. The instruction **return** k without oversupply of arguments

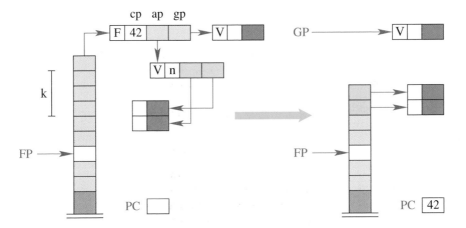

Fig. 3.23. The instruction **return** k in the case of oversupply with arguments

3.10 Recursive Variable Definitions

For a recursive variable definition

$$e \equiv \textbf{let rec } y_1 = e_1 \textbf{ and} \ldots \textbf{and } y_n = e_n \textbf{ in } e_0$$

the translation must generate an instruction sequence that accomplishes the following tasks:

- First, the local variables $y_1, \ldots, y_n$ must be allocated.
- Then the expressions $e_1, \ldots, e_n$ must be evaluated (in the case of *CBV*), or closures for these expressions must be constructed (in the case of *CBN*), to which the variables y_i must be bound.
- Finally, the expression e_0 must be evaluated and its value returned.

Here we must take into account that the variables in a *letrec* expression are defined *simultaneously*. This means, for example, that already the expression e_1 for the first variable y_1 may depend on all the variables $y_1, \ldots, y_n$. To support this, references to empty closures, called *dummy closures*, are pushed onto the stack for every variable y_i before the definitions of the variables are processed. This is realized by the MAMA instruction **alloc** n (Fig. 3.24). Later, the dummy closures will be overwritten with

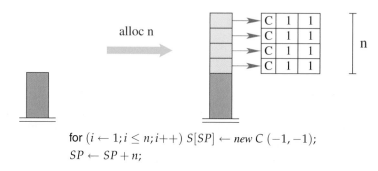

$$\text{for } (i \leftarrow 1; i \leq n; i{+}{+}) \; S[SP] \leftarrow \text{new } C \, (-1, -1);$$
$$SP \leftarrow SP + n;$$

Fig. 3.24. The instruction **alloc** n

the correct values (or the correct closures in the case of *CBN*). This is realized by the instruction **rewrite** j (Fig. 3.25). The argument j of the instruction is the difference

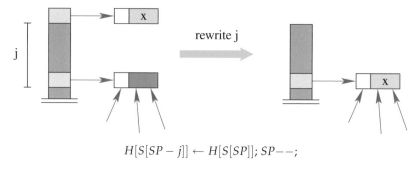

$$H[S[SP - j]] \leftarrow H[S[SP]]; \; SP{-}{-};$$

Fig. 3.25. The instruction **rewrite** j

$a_2 - a_1$ between two addresses a_1, a_2 in the stack. $S[a_1]$ consists of the reference to a dummy closure that is supposed to be overwritten with the heap object whose reference in $S[a_2]$ can be found at the top of the stack. The value $H[S[a_1]]$ is overwritten; the reference $S[a_1]$, in contrast, remains unaltered.

Overall, we obtain the following scheme for recursive variable definitions e:

$$\text{code}_V\ e\ \rho\ sl = \textbf{alloc}\ n \qquad // \text{ allocates the local variables}$$

$$\text{code}_C\ e_1\ \rho'\ (sl + n)$$

$$\textbf{rewrite}\ n$$

$$\ldots$$

$$\text{code}_C\ e_n\ \rho'\ (sl + n)$$

$$\textbf{rewrite}\ 1$$

$$\text{code}_V\ e_0\ \rho'\ (sl + n)$$

$$\textbf{slide}\ n \qquad // \text{ releases the local variables}$$

where $\rho' = \rho \oplus \{y_i \mapsto (L, sl + i) \mid i = 1, \ldots, n\}$. In the case of *CBV*, the expressions $e_1, \ldots, e_n$ are translated by the code generation function code_V as well. The reader should realize that, in the case of *CBV*, evaluating the expressions e_j must not access the values of variables y_i with $i \geq j$. This can be guaranteed for *CBV*, if recursive definitions are only allowed for *functions*.

The dummy closures are overwritten sequentially. At the start of the execution of the code for any of the e_i, as well as at the start of the execution for the main expression e_0, the stack level is equal to the stack level before the *letrec* expression increased by n.

Example 3.10.1 Consider the expression:

$$e \equiv \textbf{let rec } f = \textbf{fun } x\ y \rightarrow \textbf{if } y \leq 1 \textbf{ then } x$$
$$\textbf{else } f\ (x \cdot y)\ (y - 1)$$

$$\textbf{in } f1$$

in an empty address environment $\rho = \emptyset$ with stack level $sl = 0$. Then (for *CBV*) we obtain:

0	**alloc** 1	0	*A* :	**targ** 2	4			**loadc** 1
1	**pushloc** 0	0		...	5			**mkbasic**
2	**mkvec** 1	1		**return** 2	5			**pushloc** 4
2	**mkfunval** *A*	2	*B* :	**rewrite** 1	6			**apply**
2	**jump** *B*	1		**mark** *C*	2	*C* :		**slide** 1

where, for brevity, we have left out the code for the body of f. □

We now have all parts together to translate and execute programs of the FUL programming language with *CBV* semantics. For the implementation of *CBN*, the implementation of the instruction **eval** for evaluating closures is still missing — and of course the translation function code_C for constructing closures. This is the topic of the next section.

3.11 Closures and Their Evaluation

Closures are required for the implementation of *CBN*. With *CBN*, we cannot be sure when accessing a variable that its value is already available. If this is not the case, a stack frame must be allocated within which the expression corresponding to the variable is evaluated. This task is performed by the instruction **eval**. This instruction can be decomposed into simpler steps:

$$\textbf{eval} = \text{if } (H[S[SP]] = (C, \_, \_)) \{$$

mark0;	// allocating the stack frame
pushloc 3;	// copying of the references
apply0;	// equivalent **apply**
}	

A closure can be understood as a function without parameters, which therefore does not include the component *ap*. Evaluating a closure is analogous to evaluating the application of a function with 0 arguments. Let us discuss the different steps of the instruction **eval** in detail. If the reference at the top of the stack points to a closure, then a stack frame is allocated. This is realized by the microinstruction **mark0** (Fig. 3.26). Instead of saving a fixed address *A* as continuation address after the call as in the instruction **mark** *A*, the instruction **mark0** saves the current *PC*, which points to the first instruction after **eval**.

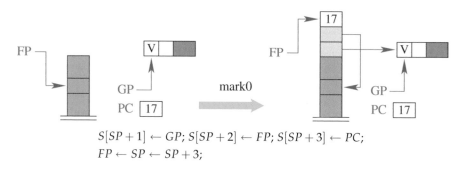

$$S[SP+1] \leftarrow GP; \ S[SP+2] \leftarrow FP; \ S[SP+3] \leftarrow PC;$$
$$FP \leftarrow SP \leftarrow SP+3;$$

Fig. 3.26. The microinstruction **mark0**

After allocation of the stack frame, the instruction **pushloc** 3 pushes the reference to the closure below the stack frame on top of the stack. The microinstruction **apply0** (Fig. 3.27) unwraps the closure on top of the stack and jumps to the address stored there in the component *cp*. This instruction behaves similarly to the instruction **apply**, which we already have seen — with the difference that a closure does not contain a vector *ap* whose references would initially have to be pushed onto the stack.

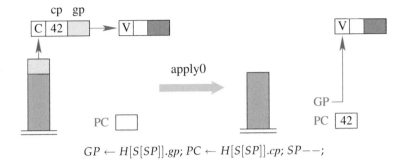

$$GP \leftarrow H[S[SP]].gp; \ PC \leftarrow H[S[SP]].cp; \ SP--;$$

Fig. 3.27. The microinstruction **apply0**

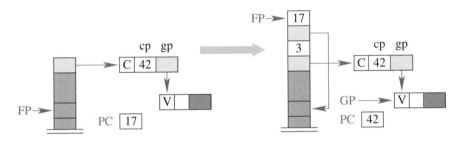

Fig. 3.28. The effect of the instruction **eval**

The combined effect of the instruction **eval** is shown in Fig. 3.28.

We now turn to the construction of closures. A closure for an expression e is constructed by first collecting the bindings for free variables into a global vector, and secondly by creating a C-object that besides the global vector contains a reference to the code for evaluating e. This code is terminated by the instruction **update**, which rewrites the closure with the computed value and pops the stack frame for the evaluation. This code is generated by the function $code_C$:

$$
\begin{aligned}
code_C \ e \ \rho \ sl = \quad &\mathsf{getvar} \ z_0 \ \rho \ sl \\
&\mathsf{getvar} \ z_1 \ \rho \ (sl+1) \\
&\ldots \\
&\mathsf{getvar} \ z_{g-1} \ \rho \ (sl+g-1) \\
&\mathbf{mkvec} \ g \\
&\mathbf{mkclos} \ A \\
&\mathbf{jump} \ B \\
A: \ &code_V \ e \ \rho' \ 0 \\
&\mathbf{update} \\
B: \ &\ldots
\end{aligned}
$$

where

$$\{z_0, \ldots, z_{g-1}\} = \text{free}(e) \qquad \text{and}$$
$$\rho' = \{z_i \mapsto (G, i) \mid i = 0, \ldots, g - 1\}$$

When generating F-objects, we already met the first part of the code generated for the expression e that aggregates the bindings for the global variables into a V-object. While F-objects are constructed by means of the instruction **mkfunval** A, the new instruction **mkclos** A is responsible for creating C-objects (Fig. 3.29).

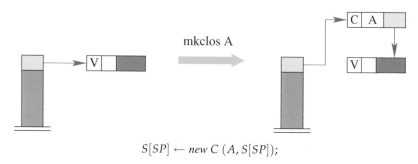

$$S[SP] \leftarrow new\ C\ (A, S[SP]);$$

Fig. 3.29. The instruction **mkclos** A

Note that we place the code for evaluating the expression e directly after the code for constructing the closure. This code refers to the address environment ρ', which records the ordering of the global variables within the global vector. Before discussing the instruction **update**, we consider an example.

Example 3.11.1 Consider the expression $e \equiv a * a$ in the address environment $\rho = \{a \mapsto (L, 0)\}$ with stack level $sl = 1$. The call $\text{code}_C\ e\ \rho\ sl$ generates the sequence:

1	**pushloc 1**	0	$A:$	**pushglob 0**	2		**getbasic**
2	**mkvec 1**	1		**eval**	2		**mul**
2	**mkclos** A	1		**getbasic**	1		**mkbasic**
2	**jump** B	1		**pushglob 0**	1		**update**
		2		**eval**	2	$B:$	**...**

In this example, the global variable a is aggregated into a global vector. The code for evaluating the expression is in the second and third columns. It is followed by the instruction **update**. The execution of this instruction terminates a possible call of **eval** for the closure that is constructed by the instructions from the first column. □

The instruction **update** is supposed to release the stack frame for evaluating the expression. Additionally, it is supposed to overwrite the C-object with the computed value. Therefore, it can be realized as a combination of two instructions (Fig. 3.30):

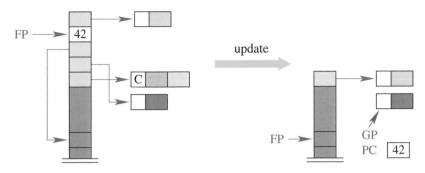

Fig. 3.30. The instruction **update**

$$\textbf{update} \quad = \quad \begin{array}{l} \textbf{popenv} \\ \textbf{rewrite } 1 \end{array}$$

The scheme for closures completes the translation of the core functional language FuL, both with *CBV* and *CBN* semantics. We note, however, that our translation only generates reasonably efficient code if we include several optimizations.

3.12 Optimization I: Global Variables

The first optimization refers to global variables. Typically, the execution of functional programs generates many *F*- and *C*-objects. Each time, this requires us to aggregate all global variables of the corresponding expression into a global vector. In order to avoid this, we may try to *reuse* already constructed vectors. This is meaningful, for instance, when translating *let* or *letrec* expressions or when generating sequences of closures for the actual parameters of function calls. Multiply used vectors can be recorded in the stack frame similar to local variables, and retrieved by means of relative addresses, which are managed in the address environment.

This optimization can be used more often if we allow global vectors that consist of *more* components than just the variables that appear in the expression. It can then be useful to allow access to the current global vector, for instance with an instruction **copyglob** (Fig. 3.31).

The advantage of this optimization is that constructing *F*- and *C*-objects becomes cheaper *more often*. The disadvantage, on the other hand, is that sometimes global vectors may contain unnecessary components. These may prevent heap objects being released although they are no longer accessible from the code — an effect which is highly undesirable as it may lead to *space leaks* and, thus, cause program executions to consume much more memory than really necessary.

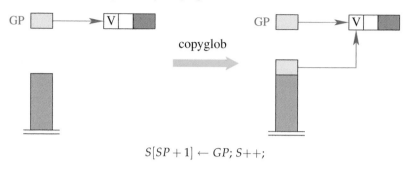

$$S[SP+1] \leftarrow GP;\ S\mathord{+}\mathord{+};$$

Fig. 3.31. The instruction **copyglob**

3.13 Optimization II: Closures

One of the main problems of programming languages with *CBN* semantics is that the construction and management of closures requires extra effort that is often unnecessary. One can safely do without constructing the closure for an expression *e*, if computing the value of *e* is not more expensive than constructing the closure itself. This is the case when the expression *e* is a constant. Therefore, we define:

$$\mathrm{code}_C\ b\ \rho\ sl = \mathrm{code}_V\ b\ \rho\ sl = \textbf{loadc } b$$
$$\textbf{mkbasic}$$

This sequence replaces:

mkvec 0		**jump** *B*	**mkbasic**	*B* : ...
mkclos *A*	*A* :	**loadc** *b*	**update**

Another case is a variable access. Variables are either bound to values or already bound to C-objects. Constructing an additional closure seems unreasonable. Therefore, we set:

$$\mathrm{code}_C\ x\ \rho\ sl = \mathsf{getvar}\ x\ \rho\ sl$$

This single instruction replaces the instruction sequence:

getvar *x* ρ *sl*	**mkclos** *A*	*A* :	**pushglob** 0		**update**
mkvec 1	**jump** *B*		**eval**	*B* :	...

Example 3.13.1 Consider the expression:

$$\textbf{let rec } a = b \textbf{ and } b = 7 \textbf{ in } a$$

With *CBN* semantics and with our optimization, $\mathrm{code}_V\ e\ \emptyset\ 0$ generates the following sequence:

0	alloc 2	3	rewrite 2	3	mkbasic	2	pushloc 1
2	pushloc 0	2	loadc 7	3	rewrite 1	3	eval
						3	slide 2

Executing this sequence should produce the basic value 7. The reader may check, however, that execution leads to a call of the instruction **eval** for a dummy closure — and therefore to a memory error.

The reason is that, in this example, the variable a is initialized by overwritting its associated dummy closure again with a dummy closure, namely the closure that was produced by the variable access to b. Even though the dummy closure for b is later overwritten by the B-object $(B, 7)$, the variable a still refers to the dummy closure. We conclude that our optimization no longer always generates correct code.   □

The problem with our optmized code generation for variable accesses only arises with recursive definitions of variables by variables where a variable y is used as the right side before the dummy closure corresponding to y has been overwritten.

Luckily, we can avoid this problem first, by disallowing at translation time cyclic variable definitions such as $y = y$ and, second, by organizing definitions $y_i = y_j$ such that the dummy closure for y_j is always overwritten before the dummy closure for y_i.

The code generation function $code_C$ can also be improved for functions e: functions are already values that need not be evaluated further. Instead of generating code that constructs the F-object only on request, we construct this object directly:

$$code_C \ (\textbf{fun } x_0 \ldots x_{k-1} \rightarrow e) \ \rho \ sl = code_V \ (\textbf{fun } x_0 \ldots x_{k-1} \rightarrow e) \ \rho \ sl$$

We leave it as an exercise to compare this code with the corresponding unoptimized instruction sequence.

After these considerations, we finish our presentation of code generation for functional programs by explaining how to generate code for the entire program.

3.14 Translating Program Expressions

The execution of a program e starts with

$$PC = 0 \qquad SP = FP = GP = -1$$

The expression e must not contain free variables. The code generated for e should determine the value of e and then execute the instruction **halt**:

$$code \ e = code_V \ e \ \emptyset \ 0$$
$$\textbf{halt}$$

It should be mentioned that the code schemes as defined so far produce *spaghetti code*. Anecdotally, it is said that an *obfuscated C contest* was once won by translating a functional program into C.

In our case, the reason for the complicated flow of control is that we placed the code for evaluating function bodies as well as closures immediately behind the instructions **mkfunval** A and **mkclos** A, respectively. This code could, equally well, be placed at other locations in the program, for example behind the instruction **halt**.

The latter code layout has the advantage that the direct jumps when constructing F- and C-objects are omitted. The disadvantage, however, is that the code generation functions become more complex, as they must maintain an additional *temporary code store* into which the swapped out program parts are accumulated.

We do not employ this approach here, but leave the jump disentanglement to a separate optimization phase.

Example 3.14.1 Consider the following program:

$$\textbf{let } a = 17 \textbf{ in } f = \textbf{fun } b \rightarrow a + b \textbf{ in } f \; 42$$

Disentanglement of the jumps of the instruction sequence with *CBN* semantics results in:

0	loadc 17	2	mark B	3 B:	slide 2	1	pushloc 1
1	mkbasic	5	loadc 42	1	halt	2	eval
1	pushloc 0	6	mkbasic	0 A:	targ 1	2	getbasic
2	mkvec 1	6	pushloc 4	0	pushglob 0	2	add
2	mkfunval A	7	eval	1	eval	1	mkbasic
		7	apply	1	getbasic	1	return 1

□

3.15 Structured Data

Every meaningful functional language offers structured data types such as tuples and lists besides simple data types such as integers and Booleans.

We begin with the introduction of *tuples*.

3.15.1 Tuples

Tuples are defined by means of constructors $(., \ldots, .)$ of arities ≥ 0 and decomposed by means of *let* expressions and *pattern matching*.

Accordingly, we extend the syntax of expressions by:

$$e ::= \ldots \mid (e_0, \ldots, e_{k-1}) \mid$$
$$\textbf{let } (y_0, \ldots, y_{k-1}) = e_1 \textbf{ in } e_0$$

for $k \geq 0$. A tuple of length k is constructed by collecting the sequence of references to its elements on the stack and by moving this sequence into the heap by means of the instruction **mkvec** k, which we have already introduced.

$$\text{code}_V \ (e_0, \ldots, e_{k-1}) \ \rho \ sl = \text{code}_C \ e_0 \ \rho \ sl$$
$$\text{code}_C \ e_1 \ \rho \ (sl + 1)$$
$$\ldots$$
$$\text{code}_C \ e_{k-1} \ \rho \ (sl + k - 1)$$
$$\mathbf{mkvec} \ k$$

In the case of *CBV*, code must be generated for evaluating the expressions e_i. The elements of a tuple are accessed by means of the expression

$$e \equiv \mathbf{let} \ (y_0, \ldots, y_{k-1}) = e_1 \ \mathbf{in} \ e_0$$

The evaluation of this construct compares the value of e_1 with the tuple pattern $(y_0, \ldots, y_{k-1})$ and then binds the variables y_i of the pattern to the corresponding components of the tuple for e_1. This procedure is called *pattern matching*. Again, we only consider non-nested patterns. In general, patterns can be built by nesting arbitrary constants, variables, and constructors. In the case of the expression e, we proceed as follows. First, code is generated for evaluating the value of the right side e_1. When executing the program, this code should deliver a V-object of length k on the heap and a reference to this vector on the stack. The references inside this vector are then pushed on top of the stack before the main expression e_0 is evaluated. Having finished with the main expression, the space for the k local variables is freed. Overall, we obtain the following translation scheme:

$$\text{code}_V \ e \ \rho \ sl = \text{code}_V \ e_1 \ \rho \ sl$$
$$\mathbf{getvec} \ k$$
$$\text{code}_V \ e_0 \ \rho' \ (sl + k)$$
$$\mathbf{slide} \ k$$

where $\rho' = \rho \oplus \{y_i \mapsto sl + i + 1 \mid i = 0, \ldots, k - 1\}$ is the new address environment for the main expression e_0.

For pushing the components of a vector of length $k \geq 0$ onto the stack, we introduce the new instruction $\mathbf{getvec} \ k$ (Fig. 3.32). Our implementation of the $\mathbf{getvec} \ k$ instruction additionally tests whether the argument reference on top of the stack is actually pointing to a V-object of the correct length. For statically typed programming languages, this will always be the case (given that code generation is correct).

3.15.2 Lists

As an example of another *recursive* data type we look at lists. Lists are built of list-elements with the help of the constant $[\ ]$ (the empty list) and the right-associative operator "::" (the list constructor). In contrast to tuples, lists can have various forms; the comparison with patterns can, thus, also be used for *case differentiation*. This is done with the *match* expression.

Example 3.15.1 Let us look, for example, at the function *app*, which takes two lists as arguments and appends the second to the first:

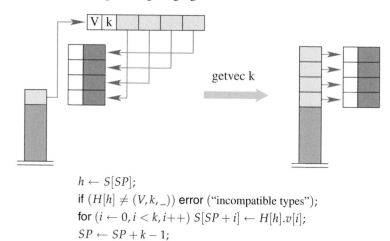

$$h \leftarrow S[SP];$$
if $(H[h] \neq (V, k, \_))$ **error** ("incompatible types");
for $(i \leftarrow 0, i < k, i++)$ $S[SP + i] \leftarrow H[h].v[i];$
$$SP \leftarrow SP + k - 1;$$

Fig. 3.32. The instruction **getvec** k

app $=$ **fun** $l\ y \to$ **match** l **with**

$$[] \quad \to \quad y$$
$$|\quad h :: t \quad \to \quad h :: (app\ t\ y)$$

$\square$

Thus, we expand the syntax of expressions e by:

$$e ::= \ldots \mid [] \mid (e_1 :: e_2)$$
$$\mid (\textbf{match}\ e_0\ \textbf{with}\ [] \to e_1 \mid h :: t \to e_2)$$

In general, patterns can be nested to any depth. Then a case differentiation might have to differentiate more than two cases. For simplicity, we here only consider patterns without nesting of constructors.

For the implementation of lists we require new heap objects (Fig. 3.33). Besides

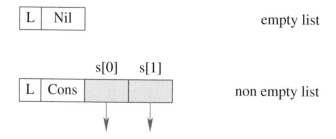

Fig. 3.33. Heap objects for lists

the tag L, which identifies them as list nodes, they consist additionally of the name of the constructor. As lists in functional programming languages are used very frequently, a real implementation uses, obviously, for L-objects a representation as compact and efficient as possible.

List nodes are allocated by means of the instructions **nil** (Fig. 3.34) and **cons** (Fig. 3.35). The call *new L (Nil)* is expected to create an L-object for an empty list

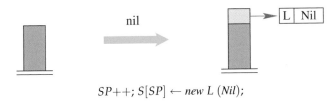

$$SP{+}{+};\ S[SP] \leftarrow new\ L\ (Nil);$$

Fig. 3.34. The instruction **nil**

in the heap and to return a reference to it. In contrast, the call *new L (Cons, h, t)* is

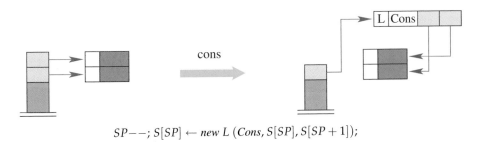

$$SP{-}{-};\ S[SP] \leftarrow new\ L\ (Cons, S[SP], S[SP+1]);$$

Fig. 3.35. The instruction **cons**

expected to create an L-object for a compound list and to store in it the references h and t.

With the two new instructions **nil** and **cons**, we translate for *CBN*:

$$\text{code}_V\ []\ \rho\ sl \quad\quad = \mathbf{nil}$$

$$\text{code}_V\ (e_1 :: e_2)\ \rho\ sl = \text{code}_C\ e_1\ \rho\ sl$$
$$\text{code}_C\ e_2\ \rho\ (sl+1)$$
$$\mathbf{cons}$$

In the case of *CBV*, the code for e_1 and e_2 is again generated by means of the function code$_V$.

It remains to generate code for the expression:

$$e \equiv \textbf{match } e_0 \textbf{ with } [\,] \rightarrow e_1 \mid h :: t \rightarrow e_2$$

Evaluating this expression, requires us to first evaluate the expression e_0. Subsequently, it must be checked whether the value of e_0 represents an L-object. If that is the case, two cases must be distinguished. If it represents an empty list, the expression e_1 must be evaluated. Otherwise, if it represents a non-empty list, the two references of the L-object must be pushed onto the top of the stack as new local variables, before evaluation may proceed to the expression e_2. Thus, we obtain (for *CBN* as well as for *CBV*):

$$
\begin{aligned}
\text{code}_V \, e \, \rho \, sl = \quad & \text{code}_V \, e_0 \, \rho \, sl \\
& \textbf{tlist } A \\
& \text{code}_V \, e_1 \, \rho \, sl \\
& \textbf{jump } B \\
A : \; & \text{code}_V \, e_2 \, \rho' \, (sl+2) \\
& \textbf{slide } 2 \\
B : \; & ...
\end{aligned}
$$

where the address environment for e_2 is given by:

$$\rho' = \rho \oplus \{h \mapsto (L, sl+1), t \mapsto (L, sl+2)\}$$

The new instruction **tlist** A performs the required tests. In the case of a *cons*, it pushes the values for the two local variables corresponding to the parts of the list (Fig. 3.36) and places the address A in the *PC* register. Note that if a data type has more than two constructors, we would rely on *indexed* jumps via a jump table (see Exercise 14) instead of a conditional to select the respective alternatives.

Example 3.15.2 The (disentangled) body of the function *app* for an address environment ρ mit $\rho(\text{app}) = (G, 0)$ looks like:

0		**targ** 2	3		**pushglob** 0	0	$C:$	**mark** D
0		**pushloc** 0	4		**pushloc** 2	3		**pushglob** 2
1		**eval**	5		**pushloc** 6	4		**pushglob** 1
1		**tlist** A	6		**mkvec** 3	5		**pushglob** 0
0		**pushloc** 1	4		**mkclos** C	6		**eval**
1		**eval**	4		**cons**	6		**apply**
1		**jump** B	3		**slide** 2	1	$D:$	**update**
2	$A:$	**pushloc** 1	1	$B:$	**return** 2			

3.15.3 Closures for Tuples and Lists

The generic scheme for code$_C$ can be optimized for tuples and lists, by constructing the corresponding values directly instead of postponing their assembly:

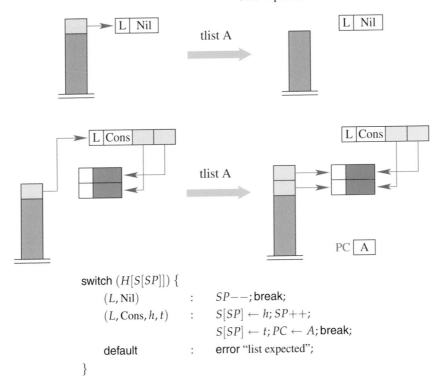

```
switch (H[S[SP]]) {
    (L, Nil)         :    SP−−; break;
    (L, Cons, h, t)  :    S[SP] ← h; SP++;
                          S[SP] ← t; PC ← A; break;
    default          :    error "list expected";
}
```

Fig. 3.36. The instruction **tlist** A

$$
\begin{aligned}
\mathrm{code}_C\,(e_0, \ldots, e_{k-1})\,\rho\,sl &= \mathrm{code}_C\,e_0\,\rho\,sl \\
&\quad\ \mathrm{code}_C\,e_1\,\rho\,(sl+1) \\
&\quad\ \ldots \\
&\quad\ \mathrm{code}_C\,e_{k-1}\,\rho\,(sl+k-1) \\
&\quad\ \mathbf{mkvec}\ k \\
\mathrm{code}_C\,[\,]\,\rho\,sl &= \mathbf{nil} \\
\mathrm{code}_C\,(e_1 :: e_2)\,\rho\,sl &= \mathrm{code}_C\,e_1\,\rho\,sl \\
&\quad\ \mathrm{code}_C\,e_2\,\rho\,(sl+1) \\
&\quad\ \mathbf{cons}
\end{aligned}
$$

3.16 Optimization III: Last Calls

The last optimization that we discuss for functional programs is crucial for the practical efficiency of the generated code: the optimization of last calls. At least for languages with *CBV* semantics, this optimization allows us to generate code for tail-recursive functions that is (almost) as efficient as that for loops in imperative languages.

The occurrence of a call $l \equiv e'\ e_0 \ldots e_{m-1}$ is called a *last occurrence* in the expression e if the evaluation of l can produce the value of e.

Example 3.16.1 The occurrence of the expression $r\ t\ (h :: y)$ is a last occurrence in the expression:

$$\textbf{match } x \textbf{ with } [\,]\ \rightarrow y \mid h :: t\ \rightarrow r\ t\ (h :: y)$$

In contrast, the occurrence $f\ (x - 1)$ is not the last in the expression:

$$\textbf{if } x \leq 1 \textbf{ then } 1 \textbf{ else } x \cdot f\ (x - 1)$$

The result of the call must be multiplied by x before the value of the overall expression is obtained. □

There is a purely syntactic procedure that determines the set of all last calls in an expression (Exercise 15). The main observation is that last calls in a function body can be evaluated in the same stack frame. Once the actual parameters and the function of the last call have been determined, it suffices to remove that part of the stack which is no longer needed.

The optimized code for a last call $l \equiv (e'\ e_0 \ldots e_{m-1})$ in a function f with k arguments therefore executes the following steps. First, the actual parameters e_i are allocated and the function e' is determined. Then the space for the local variables together with the k used arguments of f is freed. Finally, the instruction **apply** is executed.

This discussion leads to the following translation scheme for the last call l. We first present the version for *CBN*:

$$
\begin{aligned}
\text{code}_V\ l\ \rho\ sl = {}& \text{code}_C\ e_{m-1}\ \rho\ sl \\
& \text{code}_C\ e_{m-2}\ \rho\ (sl + 1) \\
& \ldots \\
& \text{code}_C\ e_0\ \rho\ (sl + m - 1) \\
& \text{code}_V\ e'\ \rho\ (sl + m) \qquad \text{// evaluation of the function} \\
& \textbf{slide } r\ (m + 1) \qquad\qquad\ \text{// release} \\
& \textbf{apply}
\end{aligned}
$$

where $r = sl + k$ is the number of stack entries to be removed. For moving the actual parameters and function of the last call, we again rely on the instruction **slide** $a\ b$, which we introduced for the C-Machine on Page 43 in Fig. 2.30.

Example 3.16.2 The body of the function

$$r = \textbf{fun } x\ y\ \rightarrow\ \textbf{match } x \textbf{ with } [\,]\ \rightarrow y \mid h :: t\ \rightarrow r\ t\ (h :: y)$$

then is translated into:

0	**targ** 2	1		**jump** B	4		**pushglob** 0
0	**pushloc** 0				5		**eval**
1	**eval**	2	A :	**pushloc** 1	5		**slide** 4 3
1	**tlist** A	3		**pushloc** 4			**apply**
0	**pushloc** 1	4		cons			**slide** 2
1	**eval**	3		**pushloc** 1	1	B :	**return** 2

Since the old stack frame is reused, **return** 2 can only be accessed via a direct jump at the end of the alternative for []. □

3.17 Exercises

1. *Functional Programming.*
   Implement a function in OCAML that takes a number as an input and checks whether it is a prime number. The result should be a Boolean value.
2. *Functional Programming.*
   Implement the Fibonacci function by means of accumulative parameters so that it runs in linear time.
3. *Functional Programming.*
   Given the program:

   ```
   let rec x = 1
   and     f = fun y → x + y + z
   and     z = 4
   in let rec x = 2
      and     g = fun y → x + (f y) + z
      in let rec x = 3
         and     f = fun y → y
         and     z = 5
         in g 6
   ```

   What is the output of the program
   a) with static scoping?
   b) with dynamic scoping?
4. *Functional Programming.*
   Implement the following functions in OCAML (alternatively in SML), without using corresponding libraries:
   • *member* takes as arguments an element e and a list l and returns whether the element is included in the list.
   • *filter* takes as arguments a predicate p and a list l and returns a list of the elements from l for which p is true.
   • *fold_left* successively combines the elements of the list with some function starting from an initial value for the empty list. This means that:

$$fold\_left \ f \ e \ [x_1; x_2; \ldots; x_n] = f \ (\ldots(f \ (f \ e \ x_1) \ x_2) \ldots) \ x_n$$

- *mapi* takes as arguments a function f and a list l and applies f to each pair of an element from l and its position in l:

$$mapi \ f \ [x_1; x_2; \ldots; x_n] = [f \ x_1 \ 1; \ f \ x_2 \ 2; \ldots; \ f \ x_n \ n]$$

For $f \ x \ i = x + i$, the call *mapi* $f \ [3; 3; 3]$ should return the list $[4; 5; 6]$.

5. *Free Variables.*

   Determine the sets of free variables for the following FUL expressions.

   $(\mathbf{fun} \ x \rightarrow x \ y) \ (\mathbf{fun} \ y \rightarrow y)$

   $\mathbf{fun} \ x \ y \rightarrow z \ (\mathbf{fun} \ z \rightarrow z(\mathbf{fun} \ x \rightarrow y))$

   $(\mathbf{fun} \ x \ y \rightarrow x \ z \ (y \ z))(\mathbf{fun} \ x \rightarrow y(\mathbf{fun} \ y \rightarrow y))$

   $\mathbf{fun} \ x \rightarrow x + \mathbf{let \ rec} \ a = x$
   $\qquad\qquad\quad \mathbf{and} \quad x = f \ y$
   $\qquad\qquad\quad \mathbf{and} \quad y = z$
   $\qquad\qquad\quad \mathbf{in} \ x + y + z$

6. *Translation and Stack Level.*

   Consider the expression

   $$e \equiv \mathbf{if} \ x > 1 \ \mathbf{then} \ x \ \mathbf{else \ let} \ z = x + y \ \mathbf{in} \ z + z$$

   Compute $code_V \ e \ \rho \ sl$ for an address environment $\rho = \{x \mapsto (L, 1), y \mapsto (L, -1)\}$ and stack level $sl = 3$. Determine, similarly as in the examples in the text, the current stack level for each instruction.

7. *Translation of Functions.*

   Consider the expression:

   $$e \equiv \mathbf{fun} \ x \ y \rightarrow \mathbf{if} \ x = 1 \ \mathbf{then} \ y \ \mathbf{else} \ fac \ (x - 1) \ (x \cdot y)$$

   Compute $code_V \ e \ \rho \ sl$ for the address environment $\rho = \{fac \mapsto (L, 1)\}$ and stack level $sl = 5$.

8. *Addressing of Variables.*

   Introduce a new register SP_0 relative to which local variables can be addressed. For this, introduce a new instruction for accessing local variables and modify the MAMA code generation so that this new register is managed correctly.

9. *Functions With Local Variables.*

   Consider the function definition:

   $$\mathbf{fun} \ x, y, z \rightarrow \quad \mathbf{let} \ x = 1$$
   $$\mathbf{in \ let} \ a = 3$$
   $$\mathbf{in \ let} \ b = 4$$
   $$\mathbf{in} \ (a + (b + (x + (y + z))))$$

- Compute the addresses of the variables a, b, x, y, and z relative to SP_0 (the stack pointer when entering the function body).
- Compute the address environment ρ that is used for the code generation of $(a + (b + (x + (y + z))))$.
- Generate call-by-value code for the function definition. Give the current stack level for each instruction. The starting stack level is assumed to be $sl = 3$.

10. *Reverse Engineering.*

    Consider the following call-by-value code of a FUL expression:

alloc 1	getbasic	jumpz _5		
pushloc 0	pushloc 5	mark _7	_3 :	return 2
mkvec 1	getbasic	pushloc 4	_1 :	rewrite 1
mkfunval _0	sub	getbasic		mark _8
jump _1	mkbasic	pushloc 4		loadc 16
_0 : targ 2	pushloc 5	getbasic		mkbasic
pushloc 0	pushglob 0	sub		loadc 12
getbasic	apply	mkbasic		mkbasic
pushloc 2	_4 : jump _3	pushloc 4		pushloc 5
getbasic	_2 : pushloc 0	pushglob 0		apply
gr	getbasic	apply	_8 :	slide 1
jumpz _2	pushloc 2	_7 : jump _6		halt
mark _4	getbasic	_5 : pushloc 0		
pushloc 3	le	_6 :		

- Compute the stack level sl for each instruction starting with $sl = 0$.
- What does this program compute? For this, try to divide the code into meaningful blocks.

11. *Translation of Whole Programs.*

    Generate code for the following program (*CBV* and *CBN*):

$$\textbf{let rec } fib =$$
$$\textbf{if } x < 3 \textbf{ then } x$$
$$\textbf{else } fib\ (x - 1) + fib\ (x - 2)$$
$$\textbf{in } fib\ 7$$

12. *Code Optimization for Call-by-Need.*

    The code generation function according to *CBN* generates an instruction *eval* for each variable access. If the variable has already been evaluated, the *eval* instruction is redundant. Thus, for the translation of the expression $(a + a + a)$ an *eval* instruction is only required after the first occurrence of the variable a.

    Redundant *eval* instructions can be saved by enhancing the code generation function with a further argument A that provides the set of already evaluated variables. For binary operators, we have:

$$\text{code}_V\ (e_1\ \square_2\ e_2)\ p\ sl\ A = \text{code}_B\ e_1\ p\ sl\ A$$
$$\text{code}_B\ e_2\ p\ (sl+1)\ (A \cup A[e_1])$$
op$_2$
mkbasic

$$A[e_1\ \square_2\ e_2] = A[e_1] \cup A[e_2]$$

Here, $A[e]$ is the set of variables in e that definitely have to be evaluated in order to compute the value of e_1.

The code generation function for the variable access is then given by:

$$\text{code}_V\ x\ \rho\ sl\ A = \begin{cases} \text{getvar}\ x\ \rho\ sl & \text{, if } x \notin A \\ \text{eval} \\ \text{getvar}\ x\ \rho\ sl & \text{, if } x \in A \end{cases}$$

- Implement $A[e]$ for any FUL expression e.
- Modify the code generation function for FUL expressions to save redundant *eval* instructions.

13. *References and Side-Effects.*

We extend FUL with *CBV* semantics with references by introducing the following syntax:

$$e ::= \ \dots\ \mid\ ()\ \mid\ \textbf{ref}\ e\ \mid\ e_1 \leftarrow e_2\ \mid\ !e\ \mid\ e_1; e_2$$

Here, $()$ is a vector of length 0. The value of **ref** e is a new heap object that contains the value of e. The value of $e_1 \leftarrow e_2$ is $()$. However, before returning $()$, the left side e_1 is evaluated to a reference object whose content is updated with the value of e_2. The operator ! is the dereference operator which returns the value saved in a reference object. After first evaluating the first argument, an ; expression returns the value of the second argument.

(a) Extend FUL with references. For this, you will have to introduce new heap objects for references. If necessary, you may introduce new machine instructions. Finally, you should define schemes for translatng the new expressions.

(b) The ; operator has a semantic meaning also without references. Could it still be useful?

14. *Trees.*

Expend FUL with the type **tree**. **Tree**s are built out of *tree* elements by means of the constant **Leaf** and the constructors **Node1**, **Node2** and **Node3**. The constructors build a *tree* value from any value plus one, two or three *tree* values. Accordingly, we extend the syntax of expressions e by:

$$e ::= \ldots \mid \textbf{Leaf} \mid \textbf{Node1}\,(e_1, e_2)$$
$$\mid \textbf{Node2}\,(e_1, e_2, e_3) \mid \textbf{Node3}\,(e_1, e_2, e_3, e_4)$$
$$\mid (\textbf{match } e_0 \textbf{ with Leaf} \rightarrow e_1$$
$$\mid \textbf{Node1}\,(x, a_1) \rightarrow e_2$$
$$\mid \textbf{Node2}\,(x, a_1, a_2) \rightarrow e_3$$
$$\mid \textbf{Node3}\,(x, a_1, a_2, a_3) \rightarrow e_4)$$

Define the code generation function for the newly introduced expressions. In particular, introduce new heap objects of type **T**.

15. *Last Calls.*
The optimization of last calls requires that the set of occurrences of last calls in expressions is available. Recall that the call $l \equiv e'e_0 \ldots e_{m-1}$ is a last call in an expression e if the evaluation of l can produce the value for e. Give a general scheme for computing the set of all occurrences of last calls in an expression e.

3.18 List of MaMa Registers

3.19 List of Code Functions of the MaMa

3.20 List of MAMA Instructions

alloc	p. 84	**mark**	p. 78	**pushglob**	p. 72
add	p. 92	**mark0**	p. 86	**pushloc**	p. 71
apply	p. 79	**mul**	p. 66	**return**	p. 82
apply0	p. 86	**mkbasic**	p. 67	**rewrite**	p. 84
cons	p. 95	**mkclos**	p. 88	**targ**	p. 80
copyglob	p. 89	**mkfunval**	p. 75	**popenv**	p. 81
eval	p. 86	**mkvec**	p. 75	**slide**	p. 98
getbasic	p. 67	**mkvec0**	p. 80	**targ**	p. 80
getvec	p. 93	**neg**	p. 66	**update**	p. 88
halt	p. 63	**nil**	p. 95	**wrap**	p. 80
leq	p. 66				

3.21 References

One of the first virtual machines for compiling functional programming languages was the SECD-Machine of Landin [Lan64]. It was created to define the semantics of Lisp programs with static scoping and *CBV* parameter passing. The G-Machine is the first virtual machine based on programmable graph reduction. It was introduced by Th. Johnsson [Joh84]. The G-Machine and the TIM (Three Instruction Machine) [FW87] influenced the design of the MAMA. An overview of the implementation of functional languages is given in [PJ87]. The further development of the G-Machine into the *Spineless Tagless G-Machine* lays the basis for the Glasgow Haskell Compiler [Jon92]. In contrast, the compilers for CAMLIGHT, MOSCOWML and OCAML rely on the virtual machine ZINC [Ler90].

4

Logic Programming Languages

The idea of logic programming can be traced back to R. Kowalski and A. Colmerauer, who discovered, at the beginning of the Seventies, how to give an operational interpretation to expressions of predicate logic. As the computational model, the mechanical resolution method is used as suggested by J.A. Robinson in 1965.

The *clause notation* is a particularly simple format for universally quantified formulas of first-order predicate logic. For such formulas, the resolution method allows us to mechanically derive contradictions. A logic formula α results from a number of formulas S if $S \cup \{\neg \alpha\}$ is contradictory. Therefore, resolution is also useful to derive implications. Resolution for *Horn* clauses is particularly straightforward. A Horn clause formalizes a rule of how an immediate conclusion can be drawn from a finite number of premises. The basic observation is that a resolution step for a Horn clause is executed similarly to a procedure call.

Logic programs can thus be discussed in three different terminologies. For programming, one speaks about rules, procedures, alternatives of procedures, variables, and so on. For explaining basics of predicate logic, one speaks of variables, functions and predicates, terms, atomic formulas, and so on. Finally, terms such as literal, Horn clause, unification, and resolution have their origin in the mechanization of predicate logic in automated theorem proving.

4.1 The Language PROL

In the following we introduce the logic programming language that we want to translate. To explain the principles of the translation we restrict ourselves to a subset of the programming language PROLOG. We call this core language PROL (**Prol**og **Language**). In PROL, we have omitted the following concepts of PROLOG:

- arithmetic,
- the cut operator, as well as
- meta-programming and self-modifying programs, for example by adding or removing clauses.

R. Wilhelm, H. Seidl, *Compiler Design*, DOI 10.1007/978-3-642-14909-2_4,
© Springer-Verlag Berlin Heidelberg 2010

As any practical programming in PROLOG is virtually impossible without cut, we will add an implementation of this operator later. Arithmetic is addressed in Exercise 10.

A PROL program consists of a number of facts and rules, together with a query. The facts and rules define predicates. The query asks whether a particular statement is satisfiable, meaning that it is true for at least one variable assignment. Consider for instance the predicate bigger of arity 2 that is defined by the following facts:

$$
\begin{aligned}
\text{bigger}(elephant, horse) &\Leftarrow \\
\text{bigger}(horse, donkey) &\Leftarrow \\
\text{bigger}(donkey, dog) &\Leftarrow \\
\text{bigger}(donkey, monkey) &\Leftarrow
\end{aligned}
$$

With the help of this predicate we can easily define a predicate for the transitive closure of the relation bigger:

$$
\begin{aligned}
\text{is\_bigger}(X, Y) &\Leftarrow \text{bigger}(X, Y) \\
\text{is\_bigger}(X, Y) &\Leftarrow \text{bigger}(X, Z), \text{is\_bigger}(Z, Y)
\end{aligned}
$$

where the names X, Y and Z serve as variables. As in PROLOG, we follow the convention that variable names always start with a capital letter or an underscore, $\_$.

To complete our program, a query is required such as:

$$\Leftarrow \text{is\_bigger}(elephant, dog)$$

In this example, the query does not contain a variable. The answer, thus, is either yes, if the query can be derived by means of rules and facts, or no, if this is not the case. If we instead had asked:

$$\Leftarrow \text{is\_bigger}(X, dog)$$

we would be interested in possible assignments to the variable X for which the fact can be derived. Note that, obviously, multiple answers are possible.

To further simplify the format of rules and facts, we additionally assume in PROL that left-hand sides always consist of predicates applied to a sequence of pairwise distinct variables. Possibly known bindings for these variables are made explicit through (unification) equations in the body, that is, on the right-hand side of the implication. As a PROL program, our example with the second query thus looks like:

$$
\begin{aligned}
\text{bigger}(X, Y) &\Leftarrow X = elephant, Y = horse \\
\text{bigger}(X, Y) &\Leftarrow X = horse, Y = donkey \\
\text{bigger}(X, Y) &\Leftarrow X = donkey, Y = dog \\
\text{bigger}(X, Y) &\Leftarrow X = donkey, Y = monkey \\
\text{is\_bigger}(X, Y) &\Leftarrow \text{bigger}(X, Y) \\
\text{is\_bigger}(X, Y) &\Leftarrow \text{bigger}(X, Z), \text{is\_bigger}(Z, Y) \\
&\Leftarrow \text{is\_bigger}(X, dog)
\end{aligned}
$$

As another, more realistic example, consider the ternary predicate app/3 that describes the concatenation of two lists:

$$\mathsf{app}(X,Y,Z) \Leftarrow X = [\,], \ Y = Z$$
$$\mathsf{app}(X,Y,Z) \Leftarrow X = [H|X'], \ Z = [H|Z'], \ \mathsf{app}(X',Y,Z')$$
$$\Leftarrow \mathsf{app}(X, [Y,c], [a,b,Z])$$

The first rule states that the list Z is the concatenation of lists X and Y in case X is the empty list and Y is equal to Z. The second rule states that the list Z is also the concatenation of lists X and Y if X and Z both contain H as the first element, and the concatenation of the remaining part X' of X together with Y results in the remaining part Z' of Z. Note that in logic programming languages, it is common practice to use a slightly different syntax for the representation of lists: Head and body are separated by means of the infix operator $|$.

For a list with the elements $X_1, \ldots, X_n$, we occasionally use the abbreviation $[X_1, \ldots, X_n]$. In contrast to OCAML, list elements are separated by a comma, instead of a semicolon. Thus, $[\,]$ describes the empty list, $[H|Z']$ is the application of the list constructor to H and Z', and $[a,b,Z]$ is the abbreviation for $[a|[b|[Z|[\,]]]]$.

The programming language PROL allows not only queries about a result of a concatenation. The different arguments of predicates are rather (at least in principle) equivalent. Thus, rules and facts can be considered as *constraints* on the arguments that must be satisfied for a fact to be derivable. The predicate app/3, for example, formalizes what it means for a list Z to be the concatenation of lists X and Y. It is then left to the evaluation of the PROL program, to determine variable assignments that satisfy these constraints.

A PROL program p is constructed as follows:

$$t ::= a \mid X \mid \_ \mid f(t_1, \ldots, t_n)$$
$$g ::= q(t_1, \ldots, t_k) \mid X = t$$
$$c ::= q(X_1, \ldots, X_k) \Leftarrow g_1, \ldots, g_r$$
$$a ::= \Leftarrow g_1, \ldots, g_r$$
$$p ::= c_1 \ldots c_m \quad a$$

A *term* t is either an atom a, a variable X, an *anonymous* variable $\_$, or the application of a constructor f/n to terms $t_1, \ldots, t_n$. According to this convention the *arity* is an important part of a constructor.

A *goal* g is either a *literal*, that is a call of a predicate q/k for argument terms $t_1, \ldots, t_k$, or a *unification* $X = t$. In unifications, the left-hand side is always assumed to be a variable X, while the right side is an arbitrary term t.

A *clause* c consists of a *head* and a *body*. Every head is of the form $q(X_1, \ldots, X_k)$ with a predicate q/k and a list of (pairwise different) *formal parameters*. A body consists of a (possibly empty) sequence of goals.

A *query* consists of a sequence of goals. Finally, a *program* consists of a sequence of clauses, followed by a query.

The idea for the efficient implementation of PROL programs is to replace the logic view of PROL programs by a procedural view. From this perspective, we consider predicates as *procedures* that are defined by means of facts and rules. Each of these alternatives represents a *potential* body of the procedure, among which program execution may choose. Accordingly, literals in the body of a rule or in the query are considered as *procedure calls*. Note that these calls do not produce a return value.

The *values* with which our program computes are terms with or without free variables. The key operation during program execution is the *unification* of such terms. This operation might *fail*, which means that a dead end has been reached. One of the previous choices of facts or rules perhaps was wrong. Program execution therefore must return to one of these choice points and select another alternative. This process is called *backtracking*. In contrast, if unification is successful, it may *bind* previously unbound variables as a *side-effect*.

In the following we present a virtual machine, WIM, for PROL. Our design aims at simplicity and as much similarity as possible with previous machines, the C-Machine for C and MAMA for FUL. Later, we discuss several improvements that make the WIM (almost) practical. Further ideas to improve efficiency, such as the use of (virtual) registers, are not considered. As usual, we start with a discussion of the basic architecture.

4.2 The Architecture of the WIM

Like the C-Machine and the MAMA, the WIM has a *program store C* as well as a register *PC*, the *program counter*, which points to the next instruction to be executed (Fig. 4.1). Again, we use the convention that each location in the program store can

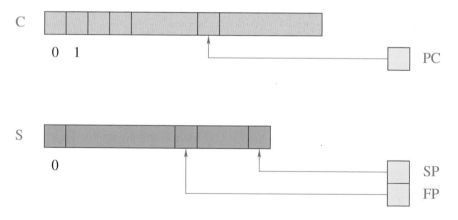

Fig. 4.1. Program store and stack of the WIM

hold one virtual instruction. The main execution cycle of the WIM is exactly the same as those of the C-Machine and the MAMA:

- load the instruction in $C[PC]$;
- increment PC by 1;
- execute the loaded instruction.

For the implementation of recursive calls as well as for local computations, a *stack* S is required. For now, we use the registers SP, the stack pointer, and FP, the frame pointer, which point into the stack. The register SP always points to the topmost occupied location in the stack, while the register FP points to the stack frame in which the local variables of the current call are located. Each individual location in S can hold single data elements, which here means addresses.

Again we also require a data structure H, the *heap*, in which representations of values are maintained (Fig. 4.2). In contrast to the heap of the virtual machine MAMA, we are now more precise regarding the implementation of this data structure. In particular, the elements in the heap, if possible, also follow a *stack discipline*. We use the register HP, the *Heap Pointer*, to point to the first free location in H. The

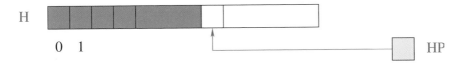

Fig. 4.2. The heap of the WIM

idea behind the stack discipline on the heap is that all recently allocated heap objects can be released in one step when backtracking occurs.

The heap objects of the WIM are summarized in Fig. 4.3. As with the MAMA, each object is tagged with its type. We differentiate A-objects for atomic terms or atoms, S-objects for structures, and R-objects for references or variables. An *unbound* variable is represented as a *self-reference*. This allows for a simple test of whether a variable is bound, that is, whether it points to another term or not.

4.3 Allocation of Terms in the Heap

Arguments of literals (calls) are constructed in the heap before being passed. Let us assume that we are given an address environment ρ, which provides for each variable X the address (relative to FP) on the stack.

A term t should be translated into a sequence $code_A\ t\ \rho$ of instructions, which constructs a representation of t in the heap and returns a reference to it on the stack.

How would the code for this look? The simplest idea is to traverse the term in *post-order*. When processing a node, the references to successors can already be found on top of the stack, just ready for creating the corresponding heap object for

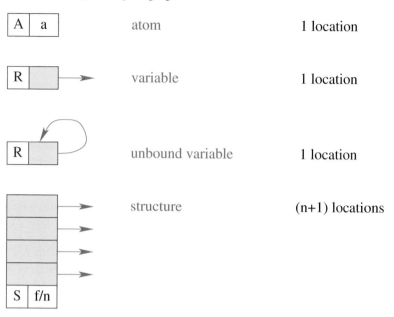

A a	atom	1 location
R	variable	1 location
R	unbound variable	1 location
S f/n	structure	(n+1) locations

Fig. 4.3. The heap objects of the WIM

the node. To realize this idea we require a WIM instruction for each possible type of node.

Example 4.3.1 Consider the following term:

$$f(g(X, Y), a, Z)$$

Here, X is assumed to have been initialized already, that is, $S[FP + \rho(X)]$ contains already a reference. In contrast, the variables Y and Z are assumed to still be unbound. Then, the heap must be extended as shown in Fig. 4.4. Note that our allocation strategy implies that references in heap locations with higher addresses always point to heap locations with lower (or equal) addresses. We will always try to achieve this direction for references whenever possible. If we could enforce this invariant throughout, younger heap objects could be released without producing references to deallocated objects (dangling references). □

Our Example 4.3.1 indicates that bound and unbound variables must be treated differently. To differentiate them, we mark occurrences of already initialized variables with a top bar ($\bar{X}$ in the example). Arguments are always initialized, but anonymous variables, on the other hand, never are. According to this discussion, we define:

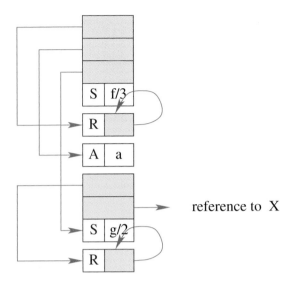

Fig. 4.4. The heap for the term $f(g(\bar{X}, Y), a, Z)$

$$\text{code}_A\, a\, \rho = \textbf{putatom } a$$

$$\text{code}_A\, X\, \rho = \textbf{putvar } \rho(X)$$

$$\text{code}_A\, \bar{X}\, \rho = \textbf{putref } \rho(X)$$

$$\text{code}_A\, \_\, \rho = \textbf{putanon}$$

$$\text{code}_A\, f(t_1, \ldots, t_n)\, \rho = \text{code}_A\, t_1\, \rho$$
$$\cdots$$
$$\text{code}_A\, t_n\, \rho$$
$$\textbf{putstruct } f/n$$

Example 4.3.2 For the term $f(g(\bar{X}, Y), a, Z)$ of Example 4.3.1 and an address environment $\rho = \{X \mapsto 1, Y \mapsto 2, Z \mapsto 3\}$, we produce the sequence:

putref 1	**putatom** a
putvar 2	**putvar** 3
putstruct $g/2$	**putstruct** $f/3$

□

In this way, code can be generated for constructing terms. We now implement the instructions that are required for this purpose.

The instruction **putatom** a creates an atom in the heap (Fig. 4.5).

The instruction **putvar** i creates a new, not initialized, variable and additionally initializes a corresponding location in the stack frame (Fig. 4.6).

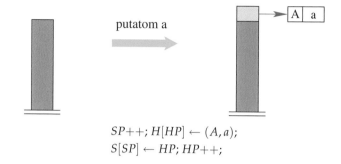

$$SP++; H[HP] \leftarrow (A,a);$$
$$S[SP] \leftarrow HP; HP++;$$

Fig. 4.5. The instruction **putatom** a

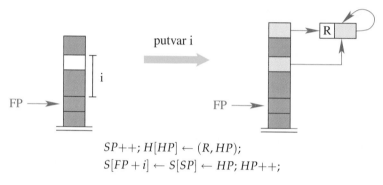

$$SP++; H[HP] \leftarrow (R,HP);$$
$$S[FP+i] \leftarrow S[SP] \leftarrow HP; HP++;$$

Fig. 4.6. The instruction **putvar** i

The instruction **putanon** creates a new unbound variable, pushes a reference to it onto the stack, but does not save a reference for it in the stack frame (Fig. 4.7).

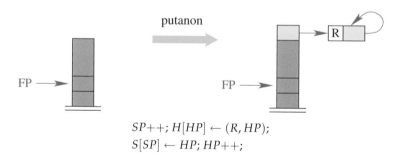

$$SP++; H[HP] \leftarrow (R,HP);$$
$$S[SP] \leftarrow HP; HP++;$$

Fig. 4.7. The instruction **putanon**

The instruction **putref** i pushes the reference from $S[FP+i]$ onto the stack and then

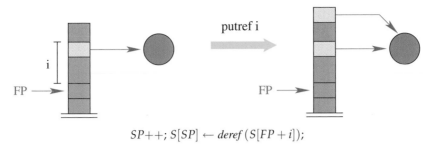

putref i

$$SP++; S[SP] \leftarrow deref\,(S[FP+i]);$$

Fig. 4.8. The instruction **putref** i

dereferences it as much as possible. For this we use the auxiliary function $deref()$:

```
ref deref (ref v) {
    if (H[v] = (R, w) ∧ v ≠ w)) return deref (w);
    else return v;
}
```

The instruction **putstruct** f/n creates an application of the constructor f/n in the heap (Fig. 4.9). Our translation scheme together with the definitions of the new

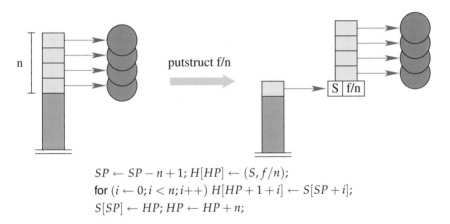

putstruct f/n

$$SP \leftarrow SP - n + 1; H[HP] \leftarrow (S, f/n);$$
$$\text{for } (i \leftarrow 0; i < n; i++) \; H[HP+1+i] \leftarrow S[SP+i];$$
$$S[SP] \leftarrow HP; HP \leftarrow HP + n;$$

Fig. 4.9. The instruction **putstruct** f/n

virtual instructions creates references that always point to lower heap addresses, not only for the example term from Example 4.3.1 but in general when building up terms.

4.4 The Translation of Literals

Literals in PROL are treated like procedure calls in imperative languages. Therefore, a stack frame is allocated for their evaluation. Representations of terms are constructed in the heap that serve as actual parameters and references to these are stored within this stack frame. Finally, control is transferred to the code for the procedure, that is, the predicate. This results in the following translation scheme for literals:

$$
\text{code}_G \ q(t_1, \ldots, t_k) \ \rho = \quad \textbf{mark } B \qquad \text{// allocate a stack frame}
$$

$$
\text{code}_A \ t_1 \ \rho
$$

$$
\ldots
$$

$$
\text{code}_A \ t_k \ \rho
$$

$$
\textbf{call } q/k \qquad \text{// call the procedure } q/k
$$

$$
B : \ldots
$$

Example 4.4.1 Consider the literal $q(a, X, g(\bar{X}, Y))$. In an address environment $\rho = \{X \mapsto 1, Y \mapsto 2\}$, our translation scheme results in:

mark B	**putref** 1	**call** $q/3$
putatom a	**putvar** 2	$B :$ ...
putvar 1	**putstruct** $g/2$	$\Box$

Before we implement the WiM instruction **mark** B, we must understand how a stack frame of the WiM is organized (Fig. 4.10). The simplest organization places first the organizational cells within the frame. Above them, the actual parameters of the literal are allocated, possibly followed by further local variables of the selected clause. As with the virtual machine for C, the parameters and local variables are addressed relative to FP. As usual, we let the current FP point to the last organizational cell. We have already identified two organizational cells. One such cell is needed for storing the current PC, the *positive continuation address*, which is the location in the code at which execution should continue if the literal has been completed successfully. This is similar to the return address in the C-Machine. One further memory cell is required for saving the contents of the register FP before the call. It turns out that, for the implementation of backtracking, four further registers and, accordingly, four more organizational cells are required.

Now we can implement the instruction **mark** B (Fig. 4.11). This instruction allocates space for six organizational cells on the stack. Then, it saves the current FP and saves B as the positive continuation address.

The instruction **call** q/k makes the register FP point to the topmost organizational cell of the stack frame and calls the k-ary predicate q/k (Fig. 4.12).

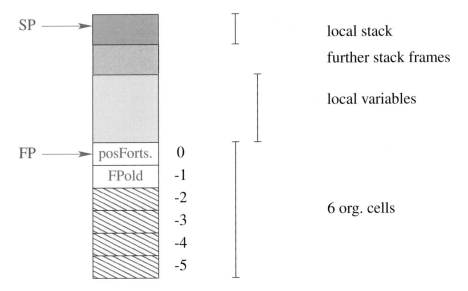

Fig. 4.10. The stack frame of the WIM

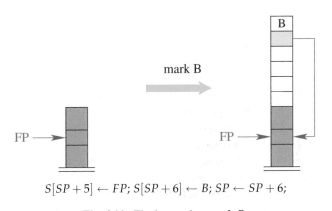

$$S[SP+5] \leftarrow FP; S[SP+6] \leftarrow B; SP \leftarrow SP+6;$$

Fig. 4.11. The instruction **mark** B

4.5 Unification

The most important operation when executing a logic program is *unification*. The goal of the unification of two terms is to find a *most general* substitution of the variables occurring within the terms such that the two terms become equal.

Example 4.5.1 Consider the two terms:

$$f(X, g(a, X)) \quad \text{and} \quad f(h(b), g(Y, Z))$$

A substitution that unifies both terms is given by:

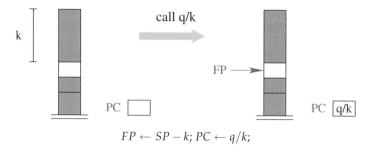

$$FP \leftarrow SP - k; PC \leftarrow q/k;$$

Fig. 4.12. The instruction **call** q/k

$$\{X \mapsto h(b), Y \mapsto a, Z \mapsto h(b)\}$$

In this example there is only one unifying substitution. This is not always the case. For the two terms:

$$f(X, g(a, X)) \qquad \text{and} \qquad f(h(Z), g(a, Y))$$

there is an infinite number of possible substitutions. One *minimal* unifying substitution, which is the one that substitutes a minimal number of variables, for these two terms is given by:

$$\{X \mapsto h(Z), Y \mapsto h(Z)\}$$

Such a minimal unifying substitution has the nice property that all other unifying substitutions can be produced from it by substituting further variables. Therefore, we call such unifying substitutions *most general unifiers*.

As the reader probably already realized, a unification may *fail*. Consider, for instance, these two terms:

$$f(X, a) \qquad \text{and} \qquad f(h(Z), g(a, Y))$$

There is no substitution of variables that makes these two terms equal. A special case is when a variable X is supposed to be unified with a term that is not itself equal to X, but contains the variable X, such as $f(X, a)$. In this case, there is also no unifying substitution – at least no unifying substitution that binds variables to *finite* terms. $\square$

Our goal is to translate a unification equation $X = t$. If the variable X on the left-hand side is not initialized, we set:

$$\text{code}_G \ (X = t) \ \rho = \textbf{putvar} \ \rho(X)$$
$$\text{code}_A \ t \ \rho$$
$$\textbf{bind}$$

The term t is constructed and then the reference object for X bound to t. This last task is realized by the instruction **bind** (Fig. 4.13.). The variable that is bound by

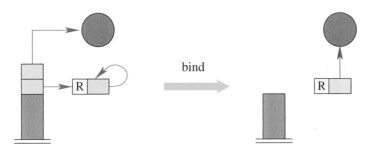

$$H[S[SP - 1]] \leftarrow (R, S[SP]); \; trail \; (S[SP - 1]); \; SP \leftarrow SP - 2;$$

Fig. 4.13. The instruction **bind**

the **bind** instruction may additionally be recorded through the call of the run-time function *trail*, which we will discuss later.

It remains to explain unification for the case that the left-hand side X is already bound. As in the case of an unbound variable, a reference to (the binding of) X is pushed onto the stack and on top of it a reference to the term t. Unifying the two terms, that is, creating the required bindings of the variables occurring in the two terms, is delegated to a dedicated instruction **unify**. This results in the following translation scheme:

$$\text{code}_\text{G} \; (\bar{X} = t) \; \rho = \text{putref} \; \rho(X)$$
$$\text{code}_\text{A} \; t \; \rho$$
$$\textbf{unify}$$

Example 4.5.2 Consider the following equation:

$$\bar{U} = f(g(\bar{X}, Y), a, Z)$$

For the address environment:

$$\rho = \{X \mapsto 1, Y \mapsto 2, Z \mapsto 3, U \mapsto 4\}$$

we have:

putref 4	**putref** 1	**putatom** a	**unify**
	putvar 2	**putvar** 3	
	putstruct $g/2$	**putstruct** $f/3$	

□

The instruction **unify** calls the run-time function *unify*() for the two topmost stack references (Fig. 4.14).

The function *unify*() of the run-time system receives as input two heap addresses and performs the unification. As an optimization, it exploits the fact that equal heap

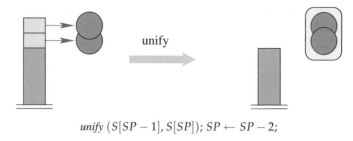

$$unify\ (S[SP - 1], S[SP]);\ SP \leftarrow SP - 2;$$

Fig. 4.14. The instruction **unify**

addresses are already unified. When binding two variables, the younger with the higher address should always be bound to the older with the lower address. When binding a variable to a term, it must be checked that this variable does not occur within the term. This check is called the *occur-check*. Additionally, all bindings that have been introduced must be recorded so that they can be reversed later if necessary. Finally, the unification may fail. In this case, backtracking is initiated.

```
bool unify (ref u, ref v) {
    if (u = v) return true;
    if (H[u] = (R, _)) {
        if (H[v] = (R, _)) {
            if (u > v) {H[u] ← (R, v); trail (u); return true; }
            else {H[v] ← (R, u); trail (v); return true; }
        } else if (check (u, v)) {
            H[u] ← (R, v); trail (u); return true;
        } else {backtrack(); return false; }
    }
    if ((H[v] = (R, _)) {
        if (check (v, u)) {
            H[v] ← (R, u); trail (v); return true;
        } else {backtrack(); return false; }
    }
    if (H[u] = (A, a) ∧ H[v] = (A, a)) return true;
    if (H[u] = (S, f/n) ∧ H[v] = (S, f/n)) {
        for (int i ← 1; i ≤ n; i++)
            if (¬unify (deref (H[u + i]), deref (H[v + i]))) return false;
        return true;
    }
    backtrack(); return false;
}
```

The unification of the terms in Fig. 4.15 sets references according to Fig. 4.16. Note that our implementation makes, whenever possible, references at higher addresses point to objects with lower addresses.

Our implementation uses three auxiliary functions. The auxiliary function *trail*() records new bindings. The auxiliary function *backtrack*() initiates the backtracking. These two functions will be discussed later. The auxiliary function *check*() implements the occur-check. It checks whether the variable in the first argument appears in the term whose representation is pointed to by the second argument. For efficiency reasons, this test is left out in some implementations. Then it is realized by:

bool *check* (ref u, ref v) { return true; }

Otherwise, it can be implemented as follows:

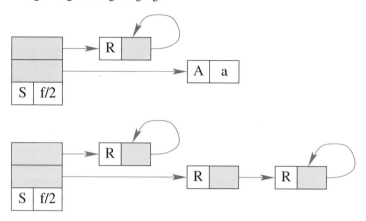

Fig. 4.15. An example input for the function *unify*()

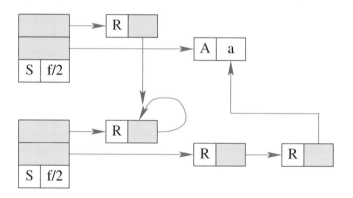

Fig. 4.16. The result of the call to *unify*() from Fig. 4.15

```
bool check (ref u, ref v) {
    if (u = v) return false;
    if (H[v] = (S, f/n))
        for (int i ← 1; i ≤ n; i++)
            if (¬check (u, deref (H[v + i]))) return false;
    return true;
}
```

Our translation of the equation $\bar{X} = t$ so far is very simple. The disadvantage is that many heap objects become garbage immediately. An improved implementation attempts to avoid creating such unnecessary objects. Only the reference to the current binding of X is pushed onto the stack, while the term t on the right-hand side of the unification equation is translated into an instruction sequence that implements the unification with t. We thus define:

$$\text{code}_G \; (\bar{X} = t) \; \rho = \textbf{putref } \rho(X)$$
$$\text{code}_U \; t \; \rho$$

for a new code function code_U. Let us first discuss how this new function translates atoms and variables:

$$\text{code}_U \; a \; \rho \; = \; \textbf{uatom } a$$
$$\text{code}_U \; X \; \rho = \; \textbf{uvar } \rho(X)$$
$$\text{code}_U \; \_ \; \rho = \; \textbf{pop}$$
$$\text{code}_U \; \bar{X} \; \rho = \; \textbf{uref } \rho(X)$$
$$\dots \; // \text{ to be continued}$$

The instruction **uatom** a implements the unification with the atom a (Fig. 4.17). The call to *trail*() records the introduced binding. If unification fails, the call to

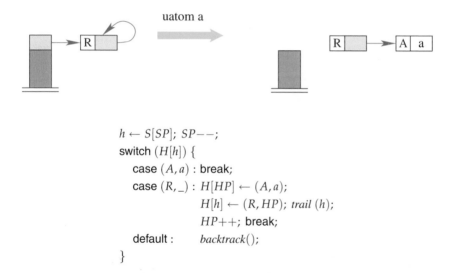

```
h ← S[SP]; SP−−;
switch (H[h]) {
    case (A, a) : break;
    case (R, _) : H[HP] ← (A, a);
                  H[h] ← (R, HP); trail (h);
                  HP++; break;
    default :     backtrack();
}
```

Fig. 4.17. The instruction **uatom** a

backtrack() initiates backtracking. As a unification with one anonymous variable always succeeds without binding any variables, it can be implemented by the instruction **pop**.

The instruction **uvar** i implements the unification with the i-th variable, provided that it is unbound (Fig. 4.18). This unification binds the i-th local variable and, thus, never fails. The instruction **uref** i implements the unification with the i-th local vari-

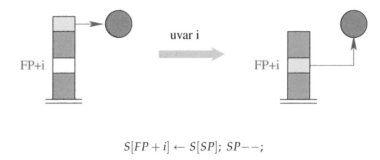

uvar i

$$S[FP + i] \leftarrow S[SP]; \; SP--;$$

Fig. 4.18. The instruction **uvar** i

able, given that it is already bound (Fig. 4.19). The reference for the i-th variable is exhaustively dereferenced before calling the function $unify()$. Since no information about the terms to be unified is available at translation time, the run-time function $unify()$ must be called.

uref i

$$unify \, (S[SP], deref \, (S[FP + i])); \; SP--;$$

Fig. 4.19. The instruction **uref** i

We now have dealt with all possibilities for simple terms. For composed terms t, the code for unification must perform a *pre-order* traversal through the term t. If thereby the current term t is unified with an unbound variable, execution must switch from comparing constructors to constructing the term t. This behavior can be achieved by:

$$\text{code}_\text{U}\ f(t_1, \ldots, t_n)\ \rho = \quad \textbf{ustruct}\ f/n\ A$$

$$\textbf{son}\ 1$$

$$\text{code}_\text{U}\ t_1\ \rho$$

$$\ldots$$

$$\textbf{son}\ n$$

$$\text{code}_\text{U}\ t_n\ \rho$$

$$\textbf{up}\ B$$

$$A: \textbf{check}\ (\text{ivars}(f(t_1, \ldots, t_n)))\ \rho$$

$$\text{code}_\text{A}\ f(t_1, \ldots, t_n)\ \rho$$

$$\textbf{bind}$$

$$B: \ldots$$

Let us discuss this translation scheme in detail. We call the section between the symbolic labels A and B the *construction block* for the term t. First assume that the reference on top of the stack, which is to be unified with (the representation of) t, represents an unbound variable X'. Then the instruction **ustruct** $f/n\ A$ jumps to the construction block. There, we check whether X' occurs in the current instance of t. If this is not the case, a representation of t is constructed followed by a redirection of the reference of X' to this representation.

The variable X' occurs in the current instance of t if and only if X' occurs in the binding of one of the already initialized variables that occur in t. In our translation scheme, the set of already initialized variables of the term t is denoted by ivars(t). The required inspection of the binding for a variable Y_j appearing in ivars(t) is realized by the instruction **check** $\rho(Y_j)$:

$$\text{check}\ \{Y_1, \ldots, Y_d\}\ \rho = \textbf{check}\ \rho(Y_1)$$

$$\textbf{check}\ \rho(Y_2)$$

$$\ldots$$

$$\textbf{check}\ \rho(Y_d)$$

The instruction **check** i checks whether the (unbound) variable at the top of the stack occurs in the term to which the variable with relative address i is bound (Fig. 4.20). If this is the case, the unification fails and backtracking is initiated. The instruction **bind** finalizes the term construction. It binds the (unbound) variable at the top of the stack to the constructed term.

Let us now discuss the unification code for a composite term $t \equiv f(t_1, \ldots, t_n)$ as a whole. This code realizes a *preorder* traversal through the term t. This traversal starts at the root of t with the instruction **ustruct** $f/n\ A$ (Fig. 4.21). The instruction **ustruct** $f/n\ A$ leaves the argument reference on the stack. It tests whether the topmost reference points to an unbound variable or a structure f/n. If neither is the case, backtracking is initiated. If the topmost reference points to an (unbound) variable, control jumps to the construction block at address A.

Otherwise, if the topmost reference points to a structure with matching constructor f/n, the process is recursively applied to the children. Afterwards, the stack is

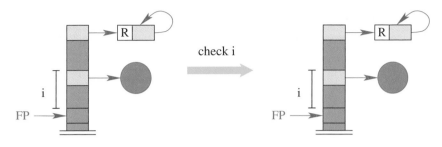

$$\text{if } (\neg check \ (S[SP], deref \ (S[FP + i]))) \ backtrack();$$

Fig. 4.20. The instruction **check** i

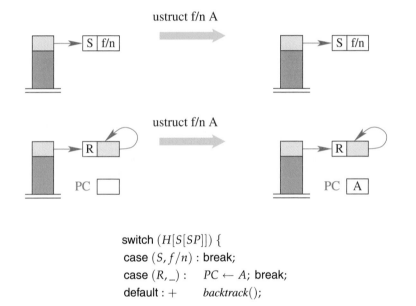

```
switch (H[S[SP]]) {
case (S, f/n) : break;
case (R, _) :    PC ← A; break;
default : +      backtrack();
```

Fig. 4.21. The instruction **ustruct** $f/n \ A$

popped and control continues at address B. The recursive descent into the i-th child is implemented by the instruction **son** i (Fig. 4.22). This instruction pushes onto the

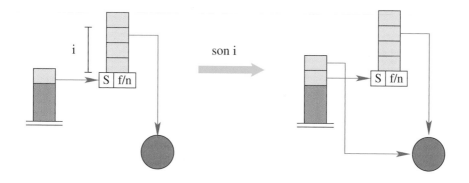

$$S[SP + 1] \leftarrow \mathit{deref}\,(H[S[SP] + i]);\; SP\text{++};$$

Fig. 4.22. The instruction **son** i

stack the i-th reference of the structure that is pointed at by the topmost reference on the stack.

The instruction **up** B is used to clean up the stack after having checked all subtrees of t (Fig. 4.23). This instruction pops the topmost reference from the stack and then sets the register PC to the address B. Within the translation scheme, this address

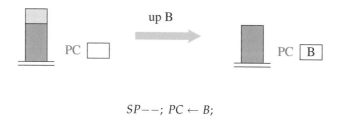

$$SP\text{--}\text{--};\; PC \leftarrow B;$$

Fig. 4.23. The instruction **up** B

B is the positive continuation address, that is, the first address after the construction block.

Example 4.5.3 For the term $f(g(\bar{X}, Y), a, Z)$ and the address environment $\{X \mapsto 1, Y \mapsto 2, Z \mapsto 3\}$ we have:

```
ustruct f/3 A₁        up B₂           B₂:  son 2         putvar 2
son 1                                      uatom a        putstruct g/2
ustruct g/2 A₂  A₂:   check 1              son 3          putatom a
son 1                 putref 1             uvar 3         putvar 3
uref 1                putvar 2             up B₁          putstruct f/3
son 2                 putstruct g/2  A₁:   check 1        bind
uvar 2                bind                 putref 1  B₁:  ...
□
```

When implementing the instructions for unification, we have made sure that the references on top of the stack are always maximally dereferenced. We have violated, however, the foremost rule of code generation: to generate for each program fragment just one instruction sequence. Indeed, for deeply nested terms, construction code is generated multiple times for the same subterms. For deep terms, the code size therefore can grow significantly. This problem, however, is not so severe in practice since very deep terms are rarely used by working PROLOG programmers.

4.6 Clauses

The code for a clause must first allocate space for the local variables of the clause. Afterwards, code is needed for evaluating the body of the clause. Finally, the stack frame should be released – at least whenever possible.

Let r be the clause $q(X_1, \ldots, X_k) \Leftarrow g_1, \ldots, g_n$. Furthermore, let $\{X_1, \ldots, X_m\}$, $m \geq k$ be the set of local variables of r. Recall that we agreed to store these variables on the stack starting from relative address 1. According to this convention, let ρ be the address environment with $\rho(X_i) = i$, for $i = 1, \ldots, m$. Then we translate:

$$\text{code}_C\, r = \textbf{pushenv}\ m \qquad //\text{reserve space for local variables}$$
$$\text{code}_G\ g_1\ \rho$$
$$\ldots$$
$$\text{code}_G\ g_n\ \rho$$
$$\textbf{popenv}$$

The new instruction **popenv** restores FP and PC and attempts to release the current stack frame. That is possible if the program execution never returns to this stack frame. We will discuss the instruction **popenv** in detail in Sect. 4.8.

In order to allocate m local variables, the instruction **pushenv** m sets the SP to $FP + m$ (Fig. 4.24).

Example 4.6.1 Consider the clause r defined by:

$$a(X, Y) \Leftarrow f(\bar{X}, X_1), a(\bar{X}_1, \bar{Y})$$

Given the address environment $\{X \mapsto 1, Y \mapsto 2, X1 \mapsto 3\}$ for the body of the clause, $\text{code}_C\, r$ produces:

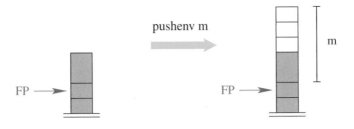

pushenv m

m

FP

FP

$$SP \leftarrow FP + m;$$

Fig. 4.24. The instruction **pushenv** m

pushenv 3	**mark** A	$A:$	**mark** B	$B:$	**popenv**
	putref 1		**putref** 3		
	putvar 3		**putref** 2		
	call f/2		**call** a/2		

□

4.7 The Translation of Predicates

Each predicate q/k is defined by a sequence of clauses $rr \equiv r_1 \ldots r_f$.

The translation of predicate q/k will certainly involve the translation of the individual clauses r_i. For $f = 1$ we have:

$$\text{code}_P\ rr = \text{code}_C\ r_1$$

If q/k is defined by multiple clauses, the first alternative must be invoked first. If this fails then the remaining alternatives are tried in sequence. For the translation of predicates it is, therefore, not sufficient just to concatenate the translations of the individual clauses. Instead, code must be generated that tentatively executes the individual alternatives and reverses their effect in case of failure. Before providing this code, we take a closer look at the backtracking of computations.

4.7.1 Backtracking

We have already seen that if unification fails, the run-time function $backtrack()$ is called. Through such a call, execution is rolled back all the way to the *dynamically* last literal where an alternative clause can be selected. We call the corresponding stack frame on the run-time stack the current *backtrack point*. To efficiently undo the variable bindings established since that point, newly applied bindings are recorded by means of the run-time function *trail()*. The calls to the function *trail()* store variables in a dedicated data structure, the *trail* (Fig. 4.25). The trail is an extra stack

Fig. 4.25. The WIM data structure *trail*

T where heap addresses of reference objects are recorded that have received a new binding. One immediate optimization is to store an address a only if its reference objects (R, b) contain bindings to too-young heap objects, that is where $a < b$. For maintaining the trail, we introduce a further register, the *Trail Pointer TP*. The trail pointer always points to the topmost used trail location.

Additionally, we require a new register BP, the *Backtrack Pointer*. It points to the current backtrack point, that is, to the last stack frame that contains a further alternative still left unexplored (Fig. 4.26).

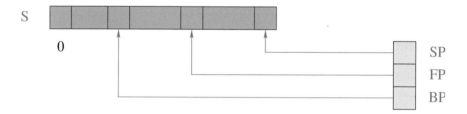

Fig. 4.26. The register BP of the WIM

Within each stack frame, we have so far saved the previous PC value, that is, the *positive* continuation address, as well as the previous FP value. This is the link to the stack frame of the caller, that is, the dynamic predecessor (Fig. 4.27). In the stack frame of a backtrack point, we additionally require the code address for the *next* alternative, that is, the *negative continuation address*, as well as the previous value of BP. These two required organizational cells have the relative addresses -5 and -4. At a backtrack point, we additionally save the previous values of the registers TP and HP. The corresponding organizational cells receive the relative addresses -3 and -2.

A call to the run-time function **void** *backtrack()* returns to the current backtrack point and continues with the negative continuation address found there (Fig. 4.28). Before the next alternative can be tried, the variable bindings that have been established since the selection of the last alternative must first be undone. This is

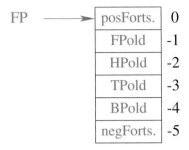

posForts.	0
FPold	-1
HPold	-2
TPold	-3
BPold	-4
negForts.	-5

Fig. 4.27. The organizational cells of the WIM

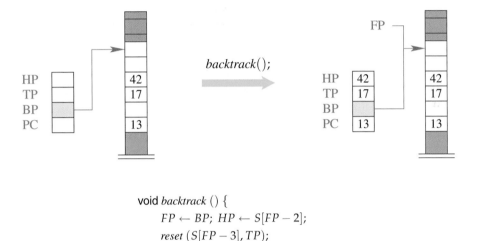

```
void backtrack () {
    FP ← BP; HP ← S[FP − 2];
    reset (S[FP − 3], TP);
    TP ← S[FP − 3]; PC ← S[FP − 5];
}
```

Fig. 4.28. The run-time function *backtrack*()

performed in two steps. First, all heap objects allocated since then, including the contained references, are deleted. For that, it suffices to reset the heap pointer to its value saved in the stack frame of the backtrack point. We would be already done with this if no old references had been bound inbetween. The addresses of the old reference objects a, however, have been recorded on the trail through calls *trail* (a). They are located on the trail at addresses $S[FP − 3] + 1, S[FP − 3] + 2, \ldots, TP$. These reference objects are *unbound* by the call *reset* $(S[FP − 3], TP)$.

The functions void *trail* (ref u) and void *reset* (ref y, ref x) are implemented by:

```
void trail (ref u) {                    void reset (ref x, ref y) {
    if (u < S[BP − 2]) {                    for (ref u ← y; x < u; u−−)
        TP ← TP + 1;                            H[T[u]] ← (R, T[u]);
        T[TP] ← u;                      }
    }
}
```

The stack location $S[BP − 2]$ contains the value of the heap pointer from the last backtrack point. The test in the function $trail()$ gives a simple criterion whether a reference should be recorded on the trail or not.

4.7.2 Putting It All Together

Assume that the predicate q/k is defined by the sequence of clauses $rr \equiv r_1, \ldots, r_f$, where $f > 1$. Code is required first to *initialize* the backtrack point. It must be ensured that the different alternatives are tried in turn. At the end, the backtrack point should be *released*. Consequently, we generate the following code:

$$\text{code}_P \; rr = q/k : \textbf{setbtp}$$
$$\textbf{try } A_1$$
$$\cdots$$
$$\textbf{try } A_{f-1}$$
$$\textbf{delbtp}$$
$$\textbf{jump } A_f$$
$$A_1: \quad \text{code}_C \; r_1$$
$$\cdots$$
$$A_f: \quad \text{code}_C \; r_f$$

Interestingly, the backtrack point is released already *before* trying the last alternative and control is directly transferred to this last alternative. The reason is that after a failure of the last alternative, control will never return to this stack frame.

Example 4.7.1 Consider the following predicate:

$$s(X) \Leftarrow t(\bar{X})$$
$$s(X) \Leftarrow \bar{X} = a$$

According to our scheme, the translation of the predicate s produces:

s/1 :	**setbtp**	A :	**pushenv** 1	B :	**pushenv** 1
	try A		**mark** C		**putref** 1
	delbtp		**putref** 1		**uatom** a
	jump B		**call** t/1		**popenv**
		C :	**popenv**		

□

New instructions are required for our translation scheme. The instruction **setbtp** creates a backtrack point. It saves the registers HP, TP and BP (Fig. 4.29). The in-

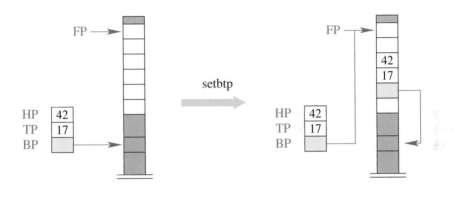

$$S[FP - 2] \leftarrow HP; \ S[FP - 3] \leftarrow TP;$$
$$S[FP - 4] \leftarrow BP; \ BP \leftarrow FP;$$

Fig. 4.29. The instruction **setbtp**

struction **try** A tries the alternative with start address A and stores the value of the PC in the current stack frame as the negative continuation address: the value of the PC is the address of the next instruction in the *try* chain (Fig. 4.30). The instruction **delbtp** finally restores the previous value of the backtrack pointer (Fig. 4.31).

4.8 The Finalization of Clauses

The only aspect left open so far when translating clauses and predicates is the instruction **popenv**. This instruction is responsible for the final treatment of the stack frame when the body of a clause has been successfully executed. Let us recall the translation of clauses:

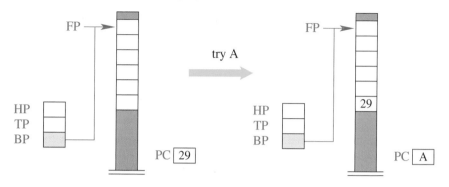

$$S[FP - 5] \leftarrow PC; \ PC \leftarrow A;$$

Fig. 4.30. The instruction **try** A

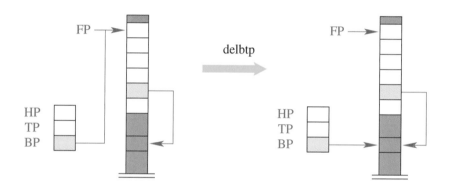

$$BP \leftarrow S[FP - 4];$$

Fig. 4.31. The instruction **delbtp**

$$\mathrm{code}_C \ r = \textbf{pushenv} \ m$$
$$\mathrm{code}_G \ g_1 \ \rho$$
$$...$$
$$\mathrm{code}_G \ g_n \ \rho$$
$$\textbf{popenv}$$

Naturally, we attempt to release the current stack frame when reaching the end of the body. This, however, is not always possible. The current stack frame can be a backtrack point with further open alternatives. Also, when executing the literals in the body of the clause, new backtrack points could have been created on top of the current stack frame. In fact, these are the only two obstacles to releasing the current stack frame. A simple test for the release of the frame is to compare the current BP with FP. If $BP < FP$, the stack frame can safely be released, otherwise it must be preserved.

This comparison is performed by the instruction **popenv** (Fig.s 4.32 and 4.33). First, the instruction attempts to release the stack frame. Then, it restores the registers FP and PC. Despite its name, the instruction **popenv** might not always pop the stack

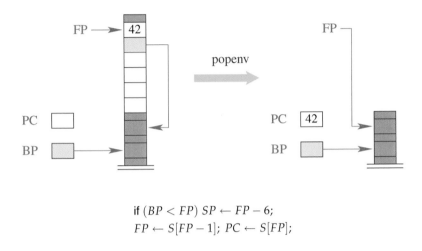

$$\text{if } (BP < FP) \; SP \leftarrow FP - 6;$$
$$FP \leftarrow S[FP - 1]; \; PC \leftarrow S[FP];$$

Fig. 4.32. The instruction **popenv** when releasing the stack frame

frame. If a stack frame of the body of a clause could not be released, still further data

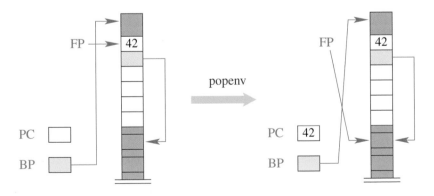

Fig. 4.33. The instruction **popenv** without release of the stack frame

may be pushed onto the top of the stack. When returning to the stack frame of the clause, the local variables may have an arbitrary distance from the Stack Pointer, but still can be addressed through the FP.

4.9 Queries and Programs

So far, we have translated all constituent parts of a PROL program. The only remaining aspect is how to translate programs as a whole. Assume that program p consists of predicate definitions $rr_1 . \ldots . rr_h$ together with the query $\Leftarrow g_1, \ldots, g_l$. The code for program p then consists of the following parts:

- code for evaluating the query $\Leftarrow g_1, \ldots, g_l$,
- an instruction **no** for failure, and
- code for the predicates rr_i.

Before program execution, we assume that $SP = FP = BP = TP = -1$ and $PC = HP = 0$. Before evaluating the query, registers SP, FP and BP must be initialized and the first stack frame must be pushed onto the stack. Afterwards, the result substitution is returned (or failure is reported):

$$
\begin{array}{rl}
\text{code } p = & \textbf{init } A \\
& \textbf{pushenv } d \\
& \text{code}_G \ g_1 \ \rho \\
& \ldots \\
& \text{code}_G \ g_l \ \rho \\
& \textbf{halt } d \\
A : & \textbf{no} \\
& \text{code}_P \ rr_1 \\
& \ldots \\
& \text{code}_P \ rr_h
\end{array}
$$

Here $\{X_1, \ldots, X_d\} = free(g_1, \ldots, g_l)$ is the set of variables in the query $g_1, \ldots, g_l$, and $\rho(X_i) = i$ for $i = 1, \ldots, d$ holds.

The instruction **halt** d terminates program execution and outputs the final bindings of variable d or initiates backtracking – if demanded by the user.

The instruction **init** A initializes SP, FP and PC and records the address A in the stack frame as the negative continuation address (Fig. 4.34). We have placed the instruction **no** at address A. This instruction is executed when the query has failed. It prints no to the standard output and halts.

Now we can translate the first complete PROL program.

Example 4.9.1 Consider the following small program:

$$
\begin{array}{lll}
t(X) \Leftarrow \bar{X} = b & q(X) \Leftarrow s(\bar{X}) & s(X) \Leftarrow \bar{X} = a \\
p \Leftarrow q(X), t(\bar{X}) & s(X) \Leftarrow t(\bar{X}) & \Leftarrow p
\end{array}
$$

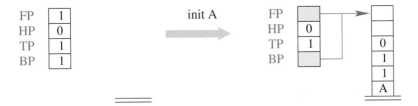

$$SP \leftarrow FP \leftarrow BP \leftarrow 5;$$
$$S[0] \leftarrow A; \; S[1] \leftarrow S[2] \leftarrow -1;$$
$$S[3] \leftarrow 0;$$

Fig. 4.34. The instruction **init** A

The translation generates:

	init N		**popenv**	$q/1:$	**pushenv** 1	$E:$	**pushenv** 1
	pushenv 0	$p/0:$	**pushenv** 1		**mark** D		**mark** G
	mark A		**mark** B		**putref** 1		**putref** 1
	call $p/0$		**putvar** 1		**call** $s/1$		**call** $t/1$
$A:$	**halt** 0		**call** $q/1$	$D:$	**popenv**	$G:$	**popenv**
$N:$	**no**	$B:$	**mark** C	$s/1:$	**setbtp**	$F:$	**pushenv** 1
$t/1:$	**pushenv** 1		**putref** 1		**try** E		**putref** 1
	putref 1		**call** $t/1$		**delbtp**		**uatom** a
	uatom b	$C:$	**popenv**		**jump** F		**popenv**

□

4.10 Optimization I: Last Goals

As with functional programs, the efficiency of the generated code can be significantly increased through simple optimizations. Consider, for instance, the predicate app/3 from the introduction:

$$\mathsf{app}(X, Y, Z) \Leftarrow X = [\,], \; Y = Z$$
$$\mathsf{app}(X, Y, Z) \Leftarrow X = [H|X'], \; Z = [H|Z'], \; \mathsf{app}(X', Y, Z')$$

The recursive call is the *last* goal in the last clause. After (successful) completion of this goal, control does not return to the current caller. We want to treat such a goal as a *last call* as we did in the translation of functional programs. If possible, no new stack frame should be allocated. Instead, the call should be evaluated in the *current* stack frame.

Consider a clause r of the form

$$q_0(X_1, \ldots, X_k) \Leftarrow g_1, \ldots, g_n$$

with m local variables, where the last goal g_n is the literal $q(t_1, \ldots, t_h)$. Let us look more closely at the cooperation between code_C and code_G:

$$
\begin{aligned}
\text{code}_C \ r = \quad &\textbf{pushenv } m \\
&\text{code}_G \ g_1 \ \rho \\
&\cdots \\
&\text{code}_G \ g_{n-1} \ \rho \\
&\textbf{mark } B \\
&\text{code}_A \ t_1 \ \rho \\
&\cdots \\
&\text{code}_A \ t_h \ \rho \\
&\textbf{call } q/h \\
B : \ &\textbf{popenv}
\end{aligned}
$$

As an optimization, we replace the **mark** B instruction with the new instruction **lastmark** and the sequence **call** q/h; **popenv** with the new instruction **lastcall** $q/h\ m$. Then, we obtain:

$$
\begin{aligned}
\text{code}_C \ r = \quad &\textbf{pushenv } m \\
&\text{code}_G \ g_1 \ \rho \\
&\cdots \\
&\text{code}_G \ g_{n-1} \ \rho \\
&\textbf{lastmark} \\
&\text{code}_A \ t_1 \ \rho \\
&\cdots \\
&\text{code}_A \ t_h \ \rho \\
&\textbf{lastcall } q/h\ m
\end{aligned}
$$

If the current clause is not the last or $g_1, \ldots, g_{n-1}$ has produced backtrack points, then $FP \leq BP$. In this case, the current stack frame cannot be released before the last call. Instead, the **lastmark** instruction must allocate a new frame with a reference to the predecessor of the current frame (Fig. 4.35). If, on the other hand, $FP > BP$, then the current stack frame can be reused for the last call. The **lastmark** instruction then does nothing.

The **lastcall** $q/h\ m$ instruction again compares the registers FP and BP (Fig. 4.36). If $FP \leq BP$, **lastcall** $q/h\ m$ behaves like an ordinary **call** q/h. If, on the other hand, $FP > BP$, the current parameters in locations $S[FP + 1], S[FP + 2], \ldots, S[FP + h]$ are replaced, and control jumps to q/h.

The difference between the original and the new addresses of the actual parameters of q/h is $SP - h - FP = m$, that is, the number of local variables in the stack frame.

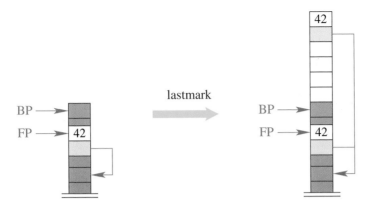

$$\text{if } (FP \le BP) \ \{SP \leftarrow SP + 6; \ S[SP] \leftarrow S[FP]; \ S[SP-1] \leftarrow FP; \ \}$$

Fig. 4.35. The instruction **lastmark**

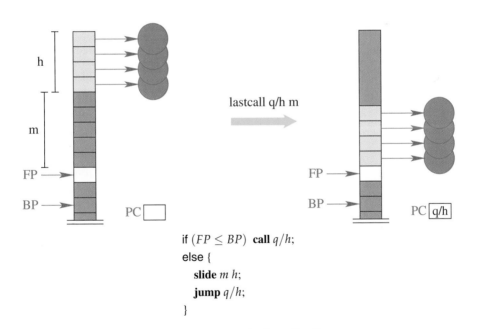

$$\text{if } (FP \le BP) \ \textbf{call } q/h;$$
$$\textbf{else } \{$$
$$\quad \textbf{slide } m \ h;$$
$$\quad \textbf{jump } q/h;$$
$$\}$$

Fig. 4.36. The instruction **lastcall** $q/h \ m$

Example 4.10.1 Consider the clause r:

$$a(X,Y) \Leftarrow f(\bar{X}, X_1), a(\bar{X_1}, \bar{Y})$$

The optimization of last goals produces for code$_C$ r in the address environment $\{X \mapsto 1, Y \mapsto 2, X1 \mapsto 3\}$:

	mark A	$A :$	**lastmark**
pushenv 3	**putref** 1		**putref** 3
	putvar 3		**putref** 2
	call $f/2$		**lastcall** $a/2$ 3

☐

If the last literal of the last clause is also the *only* literal in this clause, **lastmark** can be completely discarded, and **lastcall** q/h m can be simplified to the sequence **slide** m h; **jump** q/h.

Example 4.10.2 Consider the last clause of the predicate app/3:

$$\mathsf{app}(X,Y,Z) \Leftarrow \bar{X} = [H|X'], \ \bar{Z} = [\bar{H}|Z'], \ \mathsf{app}(\bar{X'}, \bar{Y}, \bar{Z'})$$

Here, the last goal is the only literal in this clause. Consequently, we obtain:

$A :$ **pushenv** 6		**uref** 4		**bind**
putref 1	$B:$ **putvar** 4	**son** 2	$E :$	**putref** 5
ustruct $[|]/2$ B	**putvar** 5	**uvar** 6		**putref** 2
son 1	**putstruct** $[|]/2$	**up** E		**putref** 6
uvar 4	**bind**	$D :$ **check** 4		**slide** 6 3
son 2	$C :$ **putref** 3	**putref** 4		**jump** app$/3$
uvar 5	**ustruct** $[|]/2$ D	**putvar** 6		
up C	**son** 1	**putstruct** $[|]/2$		

For the predicate app/3, we thus managed to translate the recursion in the last call into a loop.   ☐

4.11 Optimization II: Trimming of Stack Frames

As stack frames must be kept in the stack much more often than with MAMA, implementations of logic languages suffer from increased stack usage. Any possibility to systematically save space in the stack is welcome. One idea is to organize the local variables of a clause according to their *life-ranges*. A local variable X_i that is not a formal parameter and no longer occurs in the remaining sequence of goals of a clause is considered as *dead* at this program point. Dead variables can safely be removed from the stack whenever possible.

Example 4.11.1 Consider the following clause:

$$a(X, Z) \Leftarrow p_1(\bar{X}, X_1), p_2(\bar{X}_1, X_2), p_3(\bar{X}_2, X_3), p_4(\bar{X}_3, \bar{Z})$$

After the literal $p_2(\bar{X}_1, X_2)$ the variable X_1 is dead. After the literal $p_3(\bar{X}_2, X_3)$ the variable X_2 is also dead. $\square$

Assume that there is a non-last goal after which only the first m variables are alive. Then an instruction **trim** m can be inserted (Fig. 4.37). Dead local variables, how-

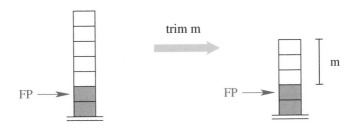

$$\text{if } (FP \geq BP) \; SP \leftarrow FP + m;$$

Fig. 4.37. The instruction **trim** m

ever, can only be removed if no backtrack points have been created whose new evaluation requires further access to the dead variables. Therefore, the instruction **trim** m compares the registers FP and BP and only removes the dead variables if $FP \geq BP$.

Example 4.11.2 Consider again the clause from Example 4.11.1:

$$a(X, Z) \Leftarrow p_1(\bar{X}, X_1), p_2(\bar{X}_1, X_2), p_3(\bar{X}_2, X_3), p_4(\bar{X}_3, \bar{Z})$$

According to the life-ranges we obtain the following order of variables:

$$\rho = \{X \mapsto 1, Z \mapsto 2, X_3 \mapsto 3, X_2 \mapsto 4, X_1 \mapsto 5\}$$

This allows us to insert *trim* instructions as follows:

pushenv 5	$A:$ **mark** B	**mark** C	**lastmark**
mark A	**putref** 5	**putref** 4	**putref** 3
putref 1	**putvar** 4	**putvar** 3	**putref** 2
putvar 5	**call** $p_2/2$	**call** $p_3/2$	**lastcall** $p_4/2\ 3$
call $p_1/2$ $B:$	**trim** 4 $C:$	**trim** 3	

$\square$

4.12 Optimization III: Clause Indexing

Often predicates are defined by case distinction on one, usually the first, argument. By taking this argument into account, many alternatives can quickly be ruled out. The advantages of a corresponding implementation are obvious: the failure of a predicate is detected earlier; backtrack points are removed earlier; and stack frames are, thus, also released earlier.

Example 4.12.1 We further clarify the situation with our predicate app/3 :

$$app(X, Y, Z) \Leftarrow X = [\,], \; Y = Z$$
$$app(X, Y, Z) \Leftarrow X = [H|X'], \; Z = [H|Z'], \; app(X', Y, Z')$$

We observe:

- If the root constructor is $[\,]$, then only the first clause can be used.
- If the root constructor is $[|]$, then only the second clause can be used.
- Any other root constructor should *fail*.
- Only if the first argument is an unbound variable both alternatives must be tried.
- □

The idea is to introduce *try* chains for any possible constructor. To keep things simple, we consider the root node of the first argument only. Depending on the result, an *indexed* jump to the corresponding chain is executed.

Assume that the predicate q/k is defined by the sequence rr of clauses $r_1 \ldots r_m$. Let tchains rr be the sequence of *try* chains corresponding to the root constructors in unifications $X_1 = t$ at the start of the body of the clauses in rr. We omit the formal definition of how the *try* chains can be extracted from rr. Instead, we illustrate the idea with an example.

Example 4.12.2 Consider again the predicate app/3 and assume that the code of the two clauses start at addresses A_1 and A_2, respectively. Then we obtain the following four chains:

VAR:	**setbtp**	// variables	*NIL:*	**jump** A_1	// atom $[\,]$
	try A_1				
	delbtp		*CONS:*	**jump** A_2	// constructor $[|]$
	jump A_2				
			DEFAULT:	**fail**	// default

The new instruction **fail** is responsible for all constructors except $[\,]$ and $[|]$:

$$\textbf{fail} \;\; = \;\; backtrack()$$

The intruction **fail** immediately initiates backtracking. □

Given the sequences tchains rr for the predicate q/k, it is straightforward to generate code for the predicate q/k:

$$\text{code}_\text{P}\ rr\quad =$$

> **putref** 1
> **getNode**   // extract the label of the root
> **index** q/k // jump to *try* chain
> tchains rr

$A_1:$ $\text{code}_\text{C}\ r_1$

...

$A_m:$ $\text{code}_\text{C}\ r_m$

The instruction **getNode** produces R if the reference at the top of the stack points to an unbound variable. Otherwise, it produces the contents of the heap object (Fig. 4.38).

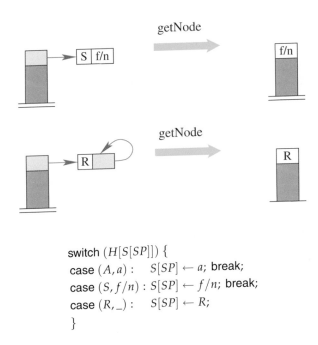

```
switch (H[S[SP]]) {
case (A, a) :   S[SP] ← a; break;
case (S, f/n) : S[SP] ← f/n; break;
case (R, _) :   S[SP] ← R;
}
```

Fig. 4.38. The instruction **getNode**

We use the instruction **index** q/k to execute an indexed jump to the corresponding *try* chain (Fig. 4.39).

The function $map()$ in the definition of the instruction **index** q/k returns the start address of the corresponding *try* chain for a given predicate and node label. We leave

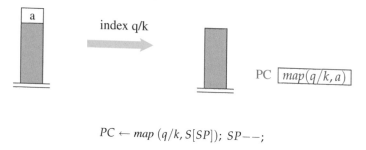

$$PC \leftarrow map\ (q/k, S[SP]);\ SP--;$$

Fig. 4.39. The instruction **index** q/k

open how the function $map()$ could be implemented. Certainly, an implementation based on hash-tables seems appropriate.

4.13 Extension: The Cut Operator

Realistic PROLOG offers an operator !, the *cut*. This operator allows us to prune the search space by explicitly limiting backtracking. Consider, for example, the following predicate:

$$\text{branch}(X, Y) \Leftarrow \text{p}(\bar{X}), !, \text{q}_1(\bar{X}, \bar{Y})$$
$$\text{branch}(X, Y) \Leftarrow \text{q}_2(\bar{X}, \bar{Y})$$

As soon as the goals *before* the cut have succeeded, all choices made before the cut are *committed*. Backtracking will only return to backtrack points *before* the evaluation of the left-hand side. In order to implement this behavior, the predecessor of the *BP* of the current stack frame is restored when the cut operator occurs. Subsequently, all stack frames above the local variables are released as no return is possible to any of these. Consequently, the cut is translated into the sequence:

prune

pushenv m

where m is the number of (still required) local variables of the clause.

Example 4.13.1 Let us consider our example:

$$\text{branch}(X, Y) \Leftarrow \text{p}(\bar{X}), !, \text{q}_1(\bar{X}, \bar{Y})$$
$$\text{branch}(X, Y) \Leftarrow \text{q}_2(\bar{X}, \bar{Y})$$

An optimized translation generates:

setbtp	A : **pushenv** 2	C : **prune**	**putref** 1	B : **pushenv** 2
try A	**mark** C	**pushenv** 2	**putref** 2	**putref** 1
delbtp	**putref** 1		**slide** 2 2	**putref** 2
jump B	**call** p/1		**jump** $q_1/2$	**slide** 2 2
				jump $q_2/2$

□

The new instruction **prune** restores the register BP (Fig. 4.40).

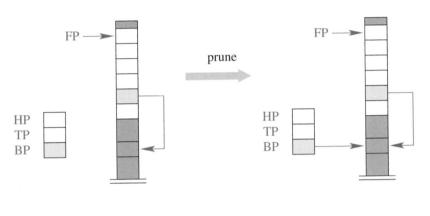

$$BP \leftarrow S[FP - 4];$$

Fig. 4.40. The instruction **prune**

Our translation scheme, however, is not always correct. If a clause is *single* in the definition of a predicate or in a *try* chain, then the BP has not been saved (at least so far not) before entering the call. Thus, the **prune** instruction cannot restore BP correctly.

To ensure that a cut is implemented correctly for a predicate defined by a single clause with cut, the instruction **setcut** is inserted before the code of that single clause. Similarly in a *try* chain consisting of a single clause with cut, **setcut** is inserted before the unconditional jump to this clause. The new instruction **setcut** saves the current value of BP.

We now have arrived at the last example of this chapter: *negation by failure*. The semantics of the programming language PROLOG follows the semantics of predicate logic formulas as long as they can be described by Horn clauses. Exact logic negation, however, cannot be expressed in PROLOG. Instead, PROLOG offers negation by failure of proof search. This kind of negation can be implemented by means of the cut operator.

Example 4.13.2 The following predicate notQ/k always succeeds when q/k fails:

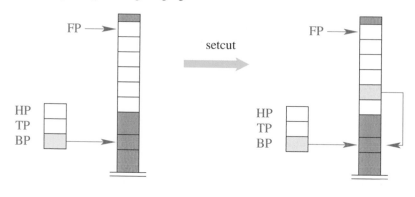

$$S[FP - 4] \leftarrow BP;$$

Fig. 4.41. The instruction **setcut**

$$\text{notQ}(X_1, \ldots, X_k) \Leftarrow \text{q}(\bar{X}_1, \ldots, \bar{X}_k), !, \text{fail}$$
$$\text{notQ}(X_1, \ldots, X_k) \Leftarrow$$

where the goal fail always fails. For notQ/k we obtain the following sequence of WIM instructions:

setbtp	A :	**pushenv** k	C :	**prune**	B :
try A		**mark** C		**fail**	
delbtp		**putref** 1		**popenv**	
jump B		**...**			
		putref k			
		call q/k			

where the instruction **popenv** in the column of label C could have been discarded. The instruction **pushenv** k in the last column is also superfluous. □

4.14 Digression: Garbage Collection

When executing a MaMa program, as well as when executing a WIM program some heap objects may at some point be no longer accessible through references. These objects are called *garbage* because they can no longer influence the remaining program execution. Their memory space can be freed and reused for storing other heap objects.

Note that the virtual machine WIM for logic programming languages already provides some sort of garbage collection. This collection, however, only refers to the space that *failed alternatives* have allocated. The reader can verify, though, that heap objects may become unreachable also during successful completion of goals.

Every practical implementation of a modern functional or logic programming language provides some method for automated *garbage collection*. Automated garbage collection is also available for object-oriented programming languages such as JAVA or C#.

In recent years, a series of interesting and efficient methods for garbage collection have been developed and evaluated in practice. A general overview, for instance, is given by [Wil92, JL96]. Garbage collection for PROLOG is addressed in [VSD02]. Here we only present the simplest method: a *copying* garbage collector and discuss how garbage collection for the WIM differs from grabage collection for the MAMA.

Conceptually, a copying garbage collector divides the memory space for the heap into two segments of which only one is used at every point in time. If the used segment is full, then all *live* objects of this segment are transferred to the unused segment. Afterwards, the roles of the two segments are exchanged.

Here, *live* objects are objects that are still needed for the remaining program execution. These are at least all objects to which references exist in the stack. Furthermore, each object is considered live if it is referenced from another live object.

The set of all live objects can therefore be determined by scanning the run-time stack and then applying an adapted algorithm for graph reachability (Fig. 4.42). Each

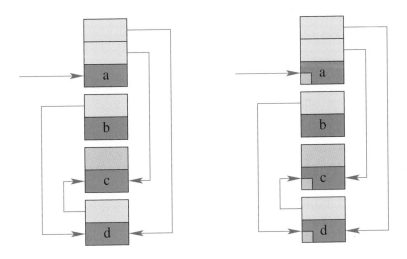

Fig. 4.42. Determining the live heap objects

object in the example has been equipped with one bit indicating whether the object has been visited or not during the reachability analysis of the garbage collector. In the next step, the live objects are copied into the fresh half of memory. This phase can actually be combined with the reachability analysis. Note, however, that when objects are literally copied, all references contained in such objects still will point to the old half of memory. Therefore, the old location of each copied object is overwritten with a *forwarding reference* to the location of the copied object in the new half of memory (Fig. 4.43).

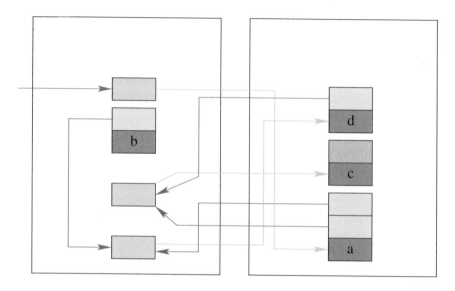

Fig. 4.43. Memory state after copying the live heap objects

After this phase, all references of the copied objects point to the forwarding references in the old half of memory. Now, the stack as well as all copied objects must be visited once more to correct the references to copied objects (Fig. 4.44). The references in the stack can be corrected directly when copying the live heap objects. The same holds true for references in heap objects that point to heap objects that have already been copied. In the final step, the roles of old and new memory halves are exchanged.

The presented method can be used for collecting garbage of the MAMA for functional languages. For collecting garbage of the WiM, this method is inappropriate. The reason is that garbage collection for the WiM must go together with backtracking. This means that the *relative positions* of heap objects must not change during collection. In our example, however, the sequence of heap objects was permuted. Less severe, but also important is that, after collection, not only the references of the stack, but also the references in the trail must be corrected or removed from the trail, if the corresponding objects are no longer reachable. This means also that all saved Heap and Trail Pointers inside the stack must be updated.

The key modification of the base algorithm for garbage collection, however, is that heap objects identified as live can no longer be immediately copied (Fig. 4.45).

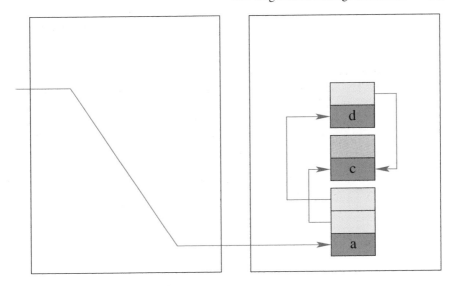

Fig. 4.44. Correction of references

Once the live heap objects have been marked, the old memory half must be traversed to copy live objects to the new half of memory in exactly the same order as they are encountered in the old half (Fig. 4.46). Subsequently, the references to heap objects

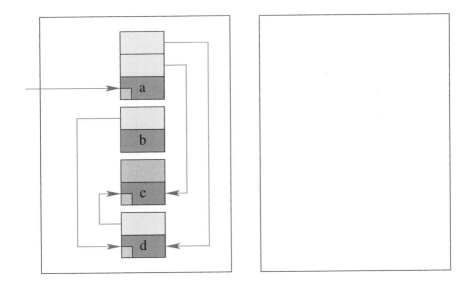

Fig. 4.45. Marking live heap objects

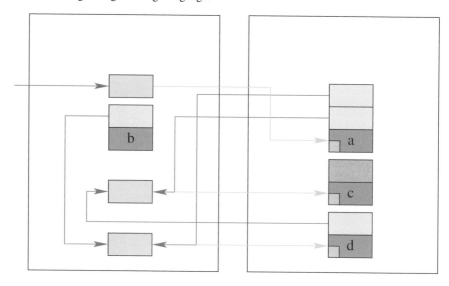

Fig. 4.46. Modified copying of live heap objects

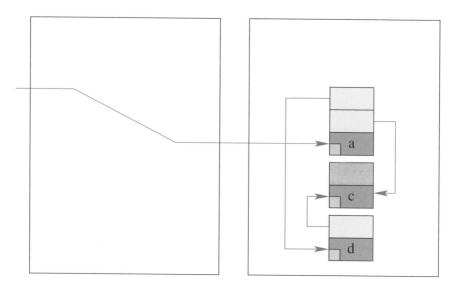

Fig. 4.47. Subsequent correction of references

are corrected as in the garbage collection for functional languages (Fig. 4.47).

This discussion should have indicated that when designing garbage collection algorithms for virtual machines like the WIM, the assumptions made by the translation schemes must be taken into account. The garbage collector for the WIM is not as efficient as the garbage collector for the MAMA: one of the reasons is that it is no longer possible to visit live heap objects only. Instead, the whole old memory segment is traversed (including the non-reachable heap objects) during the copying phase to ensure the correct order of objects after copying.

4.15 Exercises

1. *Lists in* PROLOG.   Implement the following predicates in PROLOG:
   - last/2, where the first parameter is a list and the second is the last element of this list. For instance, the following fact should be provable:

   $$last([1,2,3],3)$$

   - reverse/2 with two argument lists in reverse element order. For instance, the following fact should be provable:

   $$reverse([1,2,3,4],[4,3,2,1])$$

   - chain/2 with two lists where the second is contained in the first as a consecutive partial list. For instance:

   $$chain([1,2,3,4,5,6],[2,3,4])$$

   - remove/3 with one value and two lists as parameters. The second list is supposed to be identical to the first except for the removal of all occurrences of the first parameter. For instance:

   $$remove(2,[1,2,3,2,5],[1,3,5])$$

   Hint: You may introduce auxiliary predicates.
2. *Programming in* PROL.   Consider the following PROL program:

   $$edge(X,Y) \Leftarrow X = a, Y = b$$
   $$edge(X,Y) \Leftarrow X = b, Y = a$$
   $$edge(X,Y) \Leftarrow X = c, Y = c$$
   $$reachable(X,Y) \Leftarrow X = Y$$
   $$reachable(X,Y) \Leftarrow edge(X,Z), reachable(Z,Y)$$
   $$\Leftarrow reachable(a,c)$$

   How does this program behave when executed? Explain its behavior.
3. *Translation of Terms and Goals.*   Generate $code_A$ and $code_G$ for the following terms/goals.

– $f(X, g(b, Y), g(\bar{X}, \bar{Z}))$
– $f(g(X, h(\bar{Y}, \_)), b), Z)$

In doing so, use the following address environment:

$$\rho = \{X \mapsto 1, Y \mapsto 2, Z \mapsto 3\}$$

4. *Unification.*   Check whether the following terms are unifiable. If this is the case, give the most general unifying substitutions.
   – $z(a(b(D)), d(e(F)), g(H))$ and $z(H, K, g(F))$
   – $p(f(g(X)), Y, X)$ and $p(Z, h(X), i(Z))$
   – $f(A, g(A, B))$ and $f(g(B, C), g(g(h(t), B), h(t)))$
   – $a(b, X, d(e, Y, g(h, i, Z)))$ and $a(U, c, d(V, f, g(W, i, j)))$

5. *Unification: Running Time.*   Prove that the running time for the unification of two terms can be exponential in the number of occurring variables.
   Hint: Consider the following two terms:

   $$t_1 = f(X_0, X_1, \ldots, X_n)$$
   $$t_2 = f(b, a(X_0, X_0), a(X_1, X_1), \ldots, a(X_{n-1}, X_{n-1}))$$

6. *The deref Function.*   The run-time function *deref* shortens reference chains.
   – In which cases can reference chains arise, so that *deref* has to be called recursively at least once? Give an example.
   – How long can reference chains get in the worst case?

7. *Arithmetic I.*   In PROL positive integer numbers can be defined as (repeated) *successors of 0*:

   $$0 \equiv 0$$
   $$1 \equiv succ(0)$$
   $$2 \equiv succ(succ(0))$$
   $$3 \equiv succ(succ(succ(0)))$$
   $$\ldots$$

   – Implement predicates **greater/2**, **add/3** and **mul/3** for the corresponding mathematical predicates.

   For instance, the following fact should be provable:

   $$\mathbf{greater}(succ(succ(succ(0))), succ(0))$$

   and also:

   $$\mathbf{add}(succ(succ(0)), succ(0), succ(succ(succ(0))))$$

   – Translate the clauses of the predicate **add/3** into WIM code.

8. *Who Is a Liar?.*   Given the following PROL program:

$$\begin{aligned}
\mathsf{isLiar}(X, Y) &\Leftarrow X = true, Y = lie \\
\mathsf{isLiar}(X, Y) &\Leftarrow X = lie, Y = true \\
\mathsf{bothLie}(X, Y, Z) &\Leftarrow X = true, Y = lie, Z = lie \\
\mathsf{bothLie}(X, Y, Z) &\Leftarrow X = lie, Y = lie, Z = true \\
\mathsf{bothLie}(X, Y, Z) &\Leftarrow X = lie, Y = true, Z = lie \\
\mathsf{bothLie}(X, Y, Z) &\Leftarrow X = lie, Y = true, Z = true \\
\mathsf{findLiar}(P, T, F) &\Leftarrow \mathsf{isLiar}(P, T), \\
&\quad\quad \mathsf{isLiar}(T, F), \\
&\quad\quad \mathsf{bothLie}(F, P, T) \\
&\Leftarrow \mathsf{findLiar}(Peter, Thomas, Frank)
\end{aligned}$$

The literal $\mathsf{isLiar}(X, Y)$ formalizes: *X says, Y is a Liar!*
The literal $\mathsf{bothLie}(X, Y, Z)$ formalizes: *X says, Y and Z lie!*
The clause for $\mathsf{findLiar}(F, P, T)$ formalizes the situation in which *P says, T lie; T says, F lies, and F says, P and T lie.*

– Translate the program (without using indexing).
– Execute the translated program and answer the following question:
   Who is actually lying?
– Construct the try chains for bothLie/3 as required for clause indexing.

9. *Translation of Programs.*   Translate the program

$$\begin{aligned}
\mathsf{rev}(X, Y, Z) &\Leftarrow X = [\,], Y = Z \\
\mathsf{rev}(X, Y, Z) &\Leftarrow X = [H|L], \mathsf{rev}(L, [H|Y], Z) \\
\mathsf{reverse}(X, Y) &\Leftarrow \mathsf{rev}(X, [\,], Y) \\
&\Leftarrow \mathsf{reverse}(X, [4, 2, 1])
\end{aligned}$$

into WIM code. Apply the optimization of last goals.

10. *Arithmetic II.*   In PROLOG, the arithmetic operators $+$, $-$, $*$ and $/$ are interpreted as plain binary term constructors. In order to realize arithmetic, PROLOG provides a predicate is/2, which interprets the constructors and values found in a term. The goal: X is t evaluates the term t arithmetically and unifies the result of the evaluation with X.

   a) Extend the heap of WIM with the data type **int** and instructions for the unification of *int* values.

   b) Define an instruction **eval** that takes the term that is pointed at by the top of stack, and evaluates arithmetically and returns the result on top of the stack. If t contains unbound variables, atoms, or non-arithmetic constructors, **eval** outputs an error message and fails.

c) Consider, analogously as for the CMA or the MAMA, instructions that execute arithmetic operations on the stack and give a translation scheme $code_I$ for arithmetic expressions on the right side of an *is* goal.

d) Give a translation scheme for goals of the form X is t.

e) Use the new schems to generate code for the predicate:

$$\text{len}(X, L) \Leftarrow X = [\,], L \text{ is } 6 - 2 \cdot 3$$
$$\text{len}(X, L) \Leftarrow X = [\_|R], \text{len}(R, L'), L \text{ is } L' + 1$$

4.16 List of WIM Registers

4.17 List of Code Functions of the WIM

4.18 List of WIM Instructions

4.19 References

Introductory books on programming in PROLOG include [CM03], [Han86] and [KBS86]. [SS94] and [MW88] contain, in addition to chapters on programming methods, also chapters on the interpretation and compilation of PROLOG programs. The basics of logic programming are presented in [Llo87], [Apt90] and [Bez88].

David H.D. Warren describes in [War77] an early virtual machine for PROLOG. It still uses *structure sharing* instead of *structure copying*. The WAM (Warren Abstract Machine), the basis for most available PROLOG implementations, was defined in [War83]. It is explained didactically in a step-by-step way in [AK91].

Further developments of virtual machines for PROLOG are the basis of modern programming systems based on PROLOG, such as SWI-PROLOG [SWD05], SICSTUS-PROLOG [SIC06] and ECLIPSE [AW06]. They also provide the starting point for implementing functional-logic languages like CURRY [HS99].

5

Object-Oriented Programming Languages

Since software systems are becoming bigger and more complex, the necessity arises to make the development of such systems more efficient and transparent. One hope is to compose software systems out of ready-made standard components, as already done today for hardware systems (and most products of daily life, such as cars, washing machines, etc.). Attempts to reach this goal are based on ideas like:

- modularization,
- reusability of modules,
- extensibility of modules, and
- abstraction.

Object-oriented languages offer promising possibilities in these categories. Object-orientation is, thus, seen today as an important paradigm for coping with the complexity of software systems. In this chapter, we outline the most important concepts of object-oriented languages.

5.1 Concepts of Object-Oriented Languages

Object-oriented languages are more closely related to imperative languages than to functional or logic programming languages. Typically, they use the same execution model as imperative languages: a variant of the von Neumann computer; where a possibly complex state is changed according to an explicit flow of control. Thus, object-oriented languages can be seen as an extension of imperative languages where new concepts are added to common concepts such as variables, arrays, structures, pointers, and functions. The extensions are abstraction mechanisms and possibilities for modularization.

5.1.1 Objects

Imperative programming languages already offer functional abstractions; a possibly complex computation can be *wrapped* into a function (procedure) and be invoked

R. Wilhelm, H. Seidl, *Compiler Design*, DOI 10.1007/978-3-642-14909-2_5,

when needed. These main modularization entities are well suited as long as the complexity of data is negligible compared to that of computations. For tasks whose description and efficient solution requires us to use complex data structures, functions alone may not provide the right granularity of modularization. An adequate concept of abstraction to efficiently develop such programs should allow the encapsulation of data structures together with the associated operations. This is called *data abstraction*.

The basic concept of object-oriented languages is the *object*. An object has an object state that consists of the current values of a collection of *attributes*. Additionally, it is equipped with a set of functions that operate on this state, the *object methods*. We call the attributes and methods of an object its *members*. Thus, an object provides *encapulation* of data in its state and ties them together with the operations accessing these data. The most basic operation of object-oriented languages is the invocation of a method f for an object o, with a sequence of parameters $e_1, \ldots, e_k$, often written as $o.f(e_1, \ldots, e_k)$. For this operation, the object o is central; the method f is subordinate to o as its component. This object-orientation gave this class of languages its name.

5.1.2 Object Classes

To make program development safer and more efficient, it is desirable that inconsistencies and errors in programs be detected as early and as reliably as possible. Compilers contribute here as they inspect the parts of programs in detail. The checks of consistency and absence of errors as provided by compilers cannot be complete, as they necessarily operate with partial specifications only. An important part of these specifications are type systems, as formalized by the language designers.

(Static) type information consists of declarations for the names used in a program. It determines which run-time objects bound to these names belong to a given *type*. The type stands for a set of acceptable values. It determines which operations can be applied. Compilers can use type information to

- recognize inconsistencies,
- resolve ambiguities in the invocation of operators,
- insert automatic type conversions, and
- generate more efficient code.

Static type information, that is, type information known to the compiler, is important for generating efficient and reliable programs.

With some notable exceptions such as SMALLTALK-80, most modern object-oriented languages provide static typing. Languages like C++, JAVA and C# extend the known type concepts of imperative languages such as PASCAL and C. Their types are called *object classes*, or simply *classes*. An object class determines the attributes and methods that an object must provide in order to belong to this class. The types of attributes and the prototypes of methods (types for return value and parameters) are specified by the programmer. Some object-oriented languages, such as EIFFEL, allow further specifications for methods as, for example, pre- and post-conditions. In this way, the (semantic) meaning of a method can be specified in greater detail. Often, the class also defines the methods; but these definitions can possibly be *overloaded*. Objects that have further members beside the required ones can possibly belong to that class as well.

The object class is the concept for data abstraction provided by object-oriented languages. It serves as a *generator* for objects, which are its *instances*.

5.1.3 Inheritance

The term *inheritance* refers to the incorporation of all members of a class B into a new class A. Class A can additionally define members and overwrite methods of B. If A inherits from B, then A is called a *derived class*, or *subclass*, of B; B is called the *base class*, or also *superclass*, of A.

Inheritance significantly simplifies to create extensions and variations of classes. Through the organization in inheritance hierarchies, class libraries can be structured by providing different layers of abstraction.

The concept of inheritance allows us, in a simple way, to reuse parts of an existing implementation, to extend it and, if needed, to locally adjust it to specific requirements or conditions by modifying individual methods. Often, it is also possible to define *abstract* classes. Abstract classes are classes with methods that are not yet implemented. Abstract classes do not have instances, that is, objects of such a class must belong to concrete subclasses. This introduces a similar flexibility as in natural languages through abstract terms and different abstraction levels. Whatever can be formulated at a higher abstraction level, has a wider degree of applicability and, thus, a higher amount of reusability.

Typed object-oriented languages support inheritance hierarchies. If a class A inherits from class B, then the type attached to A is a *subtype* of the type of B. Each object of a subtype is automatically also an element of the supertype; a derived class becomes a subclass of the parent class. This results in the option that objects of any subtype of the specified type can appear when used as inputs (function parameter, right-hand sides of assignments) or as return values of methods. We call this the *subtyping rule*.

A restriction of this useful principle, however, must be mentioned: objects of a subclass of B may possibly contain additional members and, thus, cannot necessarily be stored within the same space as reserved for B objects. This is of course different if the programming language does not deal with objects themselves, but with references to objects only, such as the programming languages EIFFEL and JAVA: references always require the same amount of memory – independent of the class of the objects they point to. In contrast, the programming language C++ differentiates between objects and references to objects. Thus, in C++, for a parameter whose type is a class A, the *copy* constructor $A(\textbf{const } A\& \ x)$ of class A is implicitly called. This constructor should apply an adequate *type cast* to every object of a subclass of A.

We call the objects of A that are not also objects of a proper subclass the *proper objects* of A. Accordingly, we call A the *proper type* of the proper A objects. Each object belongs to one concrete type, which is the smallest type to which the object belongs. Furthermore, it is an element of each super-type of its proper type.

Based on the subtyping rule, methods and functions in object-oriented languages can accept as parameters (references to) objects with different types. This is one form of *polymorphism*.

Since inheriting classes may overload an inherited method, the subtyping rule of inheritance implies that the method f actually invoked at a method call $e.f(\ldots)$ must follow the concrete type of the object to which the expression e evaluates *at run-time*. Therefore, the compiler must generate code for invoking a method that is not yet known at compile-time. We are dealing here with a form of *dynamic binding*. The main part of this chapter provides an efficient implementation of method calls in the presence of inheritance.

5.1.4 Genericity

Strongly typed languages often force the re-implementation of the same function for different types, even if the functions only differ in the types of their parameters. These multiple function instances complicate the implementation and make programs unclear and difficult to maintain.

The type concept of object-oriented languages can save us in some cases from duplicating code due to inheritance. For one important class of problems, inheritance alone does not lead to elegant solutions. The implementation of general container data structures such as lists, stacks, or queues, has one natural parameter: the type of their contents. *Genericity* allows us to avoid multiple implementations for such data structures and their methods. It allows us to parameterize type (and function) definitions; types, possibly restricted, are again themselves permitted as parameters. A single definition for the parameterized class: list$\langle t \rangle$ can, for example, describe lists of any element type t. Lists with a specific type are produced through *instantiation* of the generic class list$\langle \textbf{int} \rangle$ declares, for example, a list that has elements of type **int**.

Genericity is supported by several object-oriented languages such as C++ and JAVA and C#. It is, however, not an invention of object-oriented languages. Genericity is also an important feature of modern functional programming languages, such as OCAML and HASKELL, and also the imperative language ADA provided already a sophisticated concept of genericity.

5.1.5 Information Encapsulation

Most object-oriented languages provide constructs through which the members of a class can be classified as either *private* or *public*. In specific contexts, private members are either completely invisible or at least not accessible. Some object-oriented languages distinguish several visibility contexts, such as within the class, in derived classes, in foreign classes, in specific classes, and so on. The language definition determines in which contexts which members are visible, readable/writable, or callable.

We will not discuss this any further, even though information encapsulation is of great importance for a clear separation between the meaning of a class and its implementation.

5.1.6 Summary

We tie together the results of our discussion so far:

- As a further modularization entity, object-oriented languages offer *object classes*. Object classes can encapsulate data together with the functions that operate on these data.
- *Inheritance* is a means for creating extensions and variants of already existing object classes.
- The type system of object-oriented languages supports inheritance: derived classes become subtypes of the base classes; their objects can be used at (almost) all locations where objects of the base class are allowed.
- *Inheritance hierarchies* introduce different abstraction layers to programs. This enables us to work at different parts of a program or system at different levels of abstraction.
- *Abstract* classes can be used in specifications. Since abstract classes can be repeatedly refined and finally realized, the transition from specification and design to implementation becomes much smoother.
- *Genericity* allows us to parameterize class definitions. Thus, generic algorithms and corresponding data structures, such as lists, stacks, or queues can be implemented independently of the data type of the elements.

Examples for object-oriented languages are C++ , EIFFEL, as well as JAVA and C#. In recent years, the object-oriented languages JAVA and C# have gained importance – among others as a basis for platform-independent software. The ancestor of object-oriented languages, SIMULA67, is an extension of ALGOL60 with object classes, simple inheritance, coroutines, and primitives to support discrete simulations. Another well-known example is SMALLTALK-80, a usually interpreted language without static typing, which provides simple inheritance where classes themselves are objects that can be modified at run-time. Further examples are OBJECTIVE-C, an extension of C in the spirit of SMALLTALK-80, and the object-oriented extensions of LISP such as LOOPS and FLAVORS.

5.2 An Object-Oriented Extension of C

As a concrete example of an object-oriented language, we choose a small subset of C++ with single inheritance only. Classes are considered as extensions of C structures. They consist of *attributes*, which are the data fields, *methods*, which may be declared as **virtual** so that they can then be overridden, as well as constructors, which ensure initialization when objects of the class are allocated.

Example 5.2.1 Consider the following definition of a class list:

```
int  count ← 0;
class  list  {
        int  info;
        list ∗ next;
        list (int x)  {
                info ← x;  count++;  next ← null;
        }
        virtual  int  last ()  {
                if  (next = null)  return  info;
                else  return  next → last ();
        }
};
```

The class consists of the two attributes *info* and *next* of types **int** and list ∗, respectively. Furthermore, there is a constructor to produce new list objects, as well as a method *last*, which returns the contents of the attribute *info* of the last list object reachable through *next* references. Because this method is marked **virtual**, it may be redefined in subclasses of list.

According to the philosophy of C++, objects need not necessarily be allocated in the heap, but can, similarly to structures, be also allocated on the stack. This is an essential difference to JAVA. In C++, JAVA objects would be considered as *references* to heap allocated C++ objects.

For simplicity, we omit details regarding visibility of individual attributes or methods. In order to obtain an executable C++ program we may declare, for instance, all components of the class as **public**.   □

In the following, we extend the implementation of C programs to classes as well as objects, and their members.

5.3 The Memory Organization for Objects

The implementation of objects aims at allocating within the object only members that differ from object to object. Methods which are not declared **virtual** are directly derived from the class of the object and, thus, need not be stored. In contrast, attributes and methods declared **virtual** cannot always be determined at compile time. In order to be able to uniformly address the attributes of one class in all subclasses, we insist during implementation that the new attributes of subclasses be always added after the attributes of parent classes. For virtual methods, on the other hand, their start addresses can only be determined from the *run-time type* of the respective objects. Their start addresses are, thus, not stored in each object itself. Instead, before program execution, for each class A a table t_A is allocated where the start addresses of the virtual methods are stored for all proper A objects. In an A object itself only a reference to the table t_A must be stored.

Example 5.3.1 Consider our definition of the class list from Example 5.2.1. The memory organization of an object of class list consists of a reference to the table for the virtual methods of the class, followed by two memory locations for the attributes *info* and *next* (Fig. 5.1).

Fig. 5.1. An object of class list

Assume that the subclass mylist is defined by:

```
class mylist : list {
        int moreInfo;
        virtual int length () {
                if (next = null) return 1;
                else return 1 + next → length ();
        }
};
```

Again we have omitted visibility details. In C++, a **public** declaration would have to be inserted before the parent class. Otherwise, the attributes and methods of the parent class could only be used within the derived class. Objects of the class mylist contain a reference to the table of virtual functions of the class mylist at relative address 0. This table differs from the table of the parent class in an additional entry for the method length. Also, a field for the attribute *moreInfo* has been added after the fields for the attributes of the parent class list (Fig. 5.2).   □

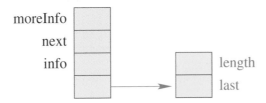

Fig. 5.2. An object of the subclass mylist

For the translation, we assume that we are given an address environment ρ_A for each class A. For every visible name x in class A, the address environment ρ_A provides a *tagged* relative address. We differentiate the following tagged entries:

global variable	(G, a)
attribute	(A, a)
virtual method	(V, a)
non-virtual method	(N, a)

When creating the address environment for methods or constructors, formal parameters and local variables are added to the address environment of the class and receive the tag L. For non-virtual methods x, $\rho_A(x)$ provides the start address of the code for x. In contrast, for virtual methods $x, \rho_A(x)$ cannot provide the start address of x, but just the relative address of the start address within the table t_A.

For the various types of variables, code is generated for computing the L-value as follows:

$$\text{code}_L \; x \; \rho \; = \; \begin{cases} \textbf{loadc } a & \text{if } \rho(x) = (G, a) \\ \\ \textbf{loadr } a & \text{if } \rho(x) = (L, a) \\ \\ \textbf{loadr } -3 & \\ \textbf{loadc } a & \\ \textbf{add} & \text{if } \rho(x) = (A, a) \end{cases}$$

The attributes of the current object are addressed relative to the reference **this** to the current object. The reference **this** is found on the stack at the fixed address -3 relative to the current frame pointer FP. As the reader may quickly calculate, this convention corresponds to passing the reference to the current object as first parameter to the method.

Instead of storing **this** in the current stack frame, we could have introduced a new register COP (*Current Object Pointer*). This register would have to be saved before calls to methods and restored afterwards. We refrained from this in order to change the architecture of the C-Machine as little as possible.

For optimizing the access to object attributes, we introduce the following derived instructions:

$$\textbf{loadmc } q \quad = \textbf{loadr } -3$$
$$\textbf{loadc } q$$
$$\textbf{add}$$

$$\textbf{loadm } q\ m \ = \textbf{loadmc } q$$
$$\textbf{load } m$$

$$\textbf{storem } q\ m = \textbf{loadmc } q$$
$$\textbf{store } m$$

where the second argument of **loadm** and **storem** is omitted whenever it is 1. These instructions could be implemented efficiently with a register COP.

5.4 Method Calls

A method call is of the form:

$$e_1.f(e_2,\ldots,e_n)$$

A call $f(e_2,\ldots,e_n)$ without declaration of the object is considered as an abbreviation of the call:

$$\textbf{this} \rightarrow f(e_2,\ldots,e_n) \qquad \text{or} \qquad (*\textbf{this}).f(e_2,\ldots,e_n)$$

We treat a call $e_1.f\ (e_2,\ldots,e_n)$ relative to the object e_1 like an ordinary function call where the object e_1 is passed as first parameter *by reference*. In the case of a virtual method f, we must take care that the method f is indirectly called through the object to which e_1 has been evaluated.

To simplify the presentation of the translation schemes, we only consider non-variable argument lists and assume that the space for the actual parameters (including the reference to the passed object) is sufficient for storing a possible return value. Then we obtain for a non-virtual method

$$\text{code}_R\ e_1.f(e_2,\ldots,e_n)\ \rho = \text{code}_R\ e_n\ \rho$$
$$\cdots$$
$$\text{code}_R\ e_2\ \rho$$
$$\text{code}_L\ e_1\ \rho$$
$$\textbf{mark}$$
$$\textbf{loadc } \_f$$
$$\textbf{call}$$

if $\rho_A(f) = (N,\_f)$ holds for the statically known class A of the expression e_1.

Note that the object to which e_1 evaluates is passed *by reference*. Technically, that means that code is generated for computing the L-value of the first parameter e_1, and not for computing the R-value, as is done for the remaining parameters.

The only difference of the translation of a call to a virtual method compared to the translation of a non-virtual method is that additionally code must be generated to determine the address of the code to be called at run-time

$$\text{code}_R \ e_1.f(e_2,\ldots,e_n) \ \rho = \text{code}_R \ e_n \ \rho$$

$$\cdots$$

$$\text{code}_R \ e_2 \ \rho$$

$$\text{code}_L \ e_1 \ \rho$$

mark

loadv b

call

if $\rho_A(f) = (V, b)$ holds for the static class A of the expression e_1. The new instruction **loadv** b computes the start address of the current implementation of f (Fig. 5.3). The start address a of the object o has been passed as the first parameter. Accordingly, it is located on the stack below the organizational cells at address $SP - 3$. The start address of o allows us to determine the start address of the virtual method table t of object o. Within this table, the start address of the method is recorded at address b.

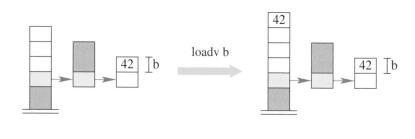

$$S[SP + 1] \leftarrow S[S[S[SP - 3]] + b]; \ SP{+}{+};$$

Fig. 5.3. The instruction **loadv** b

The instruction **loadv** b accesses the object o relative to SP. In general, such relative accesses can be implemented by means of an instruction **loadsc** q which loads the negated constant q relative to the stack pointer SP (Fig. 5.4).

As for loading (and storing) relative to the frame pointer FP, the instruction **loadsc** q allows us to implement an instruction **loads** q, which does not load the address, but the contents of the memory location $-q$ relative to SP:

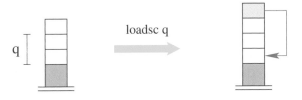

$$S[SP+1] \leftarrow SP - q; \ SP++;$$

Fig. 5.4. The instruction **loadsc** q

$$\textbf{loads } q = \textbf{loadsc } q$$
$$\textbf{load}$$

The instruction **loadv b** then can be realized by the sequence:

$$\textbf{loadv } b = \textbf{loads } 3$$
$$\textbf{load}$$
$$\textbf{loadc } b$$
$$\textbf{add}$$
$$\textbf{load}$$

Example 5.4.1 Consider the class list of Example 5.2.1. The address environment for this class is given by:

$$\rho_{\text{list}} = \{info \mapsto (A, 1), next \mapsto (A, 2), last \mapsto (V, 0)\}$$

The recursive call $next \rightarrow last()$ in the body of the virtual method $last$ is translated into the sequence:

$$\textbf{loadm } 2$$
$$\textbf{mark}$$
$$\textbf{loadv } 0$$
$$\textbf{call}$$

□

5.5 The Definition of Methods

In general, the definition of a method f of a class A is of the following form:

$$t \ f(t_2 \ x_2, \ldots, t_n \ x_n) \ \{ \ ss \ \}$$

For the implementation, we consider methods as functions with one additional first argument that consists of the reference to the current object. Within the body ss of the method, the keyword **this** refers to this reference. According to the passing convention for the first argument, the reference is located within the stack frame at relative address -3. Thus, we translate:

$$\text{code}_R \text{ this } \rho = \text{loadr } -3$$

Otherwise, the translation scheme for methods in C++ is the same as the corresponding scheme for translating function definitions in C.

Example 5.5.1 Consider again the class list of Example 5.2.1. The implementation of the method *last* results in:

_last :	enter 6	loadm 1	loadv 0
	alloc 0	storer -3	call
	loadm 2	return	storer -3
	loadc 0		return
	eq	$A:$ loadm 2	
	jumpz A	mark	

At address A, code is generated for computing the L-value of the expression $(*next)$, that is, the code for computing the R-value of *next*. This consists of the instruction **loadm** 2.

The instruction sequence for the method *last* looks familiar. The only difference to a corresponding instruction sequence for C functions is that we use specialized instructions **loadm** and **storem** to access the attributes of the current object. Also instructions **loadv** are required for determining the start addresses of virtual methods.
□

5.6 The Use of Constructors

Object-oriented languages like C++ offer the possibility to define constructors for a class A, by which a newly created object can be initialized. We distinguish two types of object creation:

(1)   *direct*, such as on the right side of an assignment

$$A\,(e_2,\dots,e_n)$$

by which the (initialized) object itself is returned as an R-value.

(2)   *indirect* on the heap

$$\textbf{new }\ A\,(e_2,\dots,e_n)$$

by which a reference to the newly created object is returned as an R-value.

First, we consider indirect object creation. We expect from an implementation that it first allocates space on the heap for the new object. Then, the fields for the virtual functions should be initialized. The call to the constructor itself is treated like a function call in C. Care must be taken that the reference to the new object is passed as the first (implicit) parameter to the constructor and that it is also left on top of the stack after completing the call. This is achieved by the following scheme:

$$\text{code}_R\ (\textbf{new}\ A\ (e_2, \ldots, e_n))\ \rho = \textbf{loadc}\ |A|$$

$$\textbf{new}$$
$$\text{code}_R\ e_n\ \rho$$
$$\ldots$$
$$\text{code}_R\ e_2\ \rho$$
$$\textbf{loads}\ m \qquad // \quad \text{load relative to } SP$$
$$\textbf{mark}$$
$$\textbf{loadc}\ \_A$$
$$\textbf{call}$$

where m is the size of the actual parameters $e_2, \ldots, e_n$, $|A|$ is size of an instance of A, and $\_A$ is the start address of the code for the constructor.

Next we consider the call of a constructor in an ordinary expression. The semantics demands that the R-value is evaluated without creating the new object in the heap. Instead, it is allocated on the stack where it is returned. Therefore, first sufficient space is allocated on the stack before the arguments of the constructor call are evaluated. Then a reference to the newly created object is passed as first argument to the constructor. This results in the following translation scheme:

$$\text{code}_R\ (A\ (e_2, \ldots, e_n))\ \rho = \textbf{alloc}\ |A|$$

$$\text{code}_R\ e_n\ \rho$$
$$\ldots$$
$$\text{code}_R\ e_2\ \rho$$
$$\textbf{loadsc}\ q$$
$$\textbf{mark}$$
$$\textbf{loadc}\ \_A$$
$$\textbf{call}$$

where $\_A$ is the start address of the constructor to be called for class A. The start address of the newly allocated object can be determined relative to the Stack Pointer. If m is the space requirement for the actual parameters $e_2, \ldots, e_n$, then the distance q to the Stack Pointer is given by:

$$q = m + |A| - 1$$

During creation of a new object, only the space occupied by the object is allocated. Initialization of the attributes as well as of the virtual function table is delegated to the constructor.

5.7 The Definition of Constructors

Finally, we consider the translation of definitions of constructors. Such a definition has the form:

$$d \equiv A\,(t_2\,x_2,\ldots,t_n\,x_n)\,\{\,ss\,\}$$

Again, the idea is not to invent new translation schemes, but to translate the definition of a constructor similarly to the definition of any method without return value. There is just one extra task: the constructor must first initialize the field for the virtual function table. This task is implemented by the macro-instruction initVirtual A:

$$\text{initVirtual } A = \textbf{loadc }\_tA$$
$$\textbf{storem } 0$$
$$\textbf{pop}$$

where $\_tA$ is the start address of the table t_A for the virtual methods of class A. Then we define:

$$\text{code } d\,\rho = \textbf{enter } q$$
$$\text{initVirtual } A$$
$$\text{code } ss\,\rho'$$

where q is the space requirement on the stack and ρ' is the address environment within the constructor A after the evaluation of the formal parameters.

Example 5.7.1 In order to complete the translation of the class of Example 5.2.1, it remains to provide the translation of the list constructor. For that, the following code is generated:

enter 3	**alloc** 0	**loada** 1	**loadc** 0
loadc _tlist	**loadr** −4	**loadc** 1	**storem** 2
storem 0	**storem** 1	**add**	**pop**
pop	**pop**	**storea** 1	**return**
		pop	

Apart from the initialization of the virtual functions table, nothing surprising can be found here. The reference to the object for which the constructor is called has address −3 (relative to FP) while the attributes of this object can be accessed through the instructions **loadm** and **storem**.   □

A constructor may call a constructor of the parent class. In C++ syntax, this constructor is declared in the header of the constructor declaration:

$$d \equiv A\,(t_2\ x_2, \dots, t_m\ x_m) \ : \ B\,(e_2, \dots, e_n)\ \{\ ss\ \}$$

A translation of this declaration must take care that the constructor of the given parent class is called before the body ss is evaluated. As the constructor of B is called for the same object as the constructor of A, it receives the reference to the current object as its object reference. Moreover, its parameters must not be evaluated relative to the address environment within the constructor A, but relative to the address environment of class A, extended by the formal parameters of the constructor of A. As the constructor of the parent class B possibly calls its own versions of virtual methods, the reference to the virtual functions table for class A is initialized only after the constructor of the parent class B has terminated.

$$
\begin{aligned}
\text{code}\ \ d\ \rho =\ &\textbf{enter}\ q \\
&\text{code}_R\ e_n\ \rho_1 \\
&\qquad \dots \\
&\text{code}_R\ e_2\ \rho_1 \\
&\textbf{loadr}\ -3 \\
&\textbf{mark} \\
&\textbf{loadc}\ \_B \\
&\textbf{call} \\
&\text{initVirtual}\ A \\
&\text{code}\ ss\ \rho'
\end{aligned}
$$

where q is the stack space required by the constructor of A, ρ_1 is the address environment for the evaluation of the actual parameters of the constructor of the class B, and ρ' is the address environment within the constructor A.

Our implementation of the allocation of new objects ensures that each constructor uses the versions of virtual methods of its own class. To achieve this, we place in each new object the reference to the actual table of virtual functions only *after* the call to the constructors of parent classes.

The problem of when to allocate the table of virtual methods during the allocation of a new object is solved differently in different programming languages. In contrast to the strategy described here, the constructor of the parent class B in JAVA may call the methods of the subclass A. Thus in JAVA, the table for virtual methods must be allocated *before* the constructor of the parent class is called.

5.8 Perspective: Multiple Inheritance

This section concludes our short introduction to the translation of object-oriented languages by a brief discussion of the concept of *multiple inheritance*. Multiple inheritance is supported by programming languages such as C++, EIFFEL and SCALA.

These programming languages allow one subclass A to inherit from multiple parent classes $B_1, \ldots, B_k$ simultaneously. Providing a meaningful semantics for multiple inheritance is already a challenging problem. The difficulties of formalizing the complex semantics of the version of multiple inheritance as provided by C++ are discussed in [WNST06]. A fundamental problem of multiple inheritance is how to resolve ambiguities arising from inheritance: different methods with the same name may be inherited, or the same parent class may contribute to a subclass A along different paths.

A trivial form of multiple inheritance is supported by the programming language JAVA. JAVA does not provide multiple inheritance in the strict sense: besides inheriting from a parent class B, a class A may only *implement* an arbitrary number of *interfaces*. An interface is an *abstract* class without its own attributes. Definitions for the methods of an interface need to be provided by its implementing subclasses. In JAVA jargon, the methods of an interface are *abstract*, in C++ jargon, *pure virtual*.

As interfaces do not have attributes, and as in the class A there is at most one implementation available for each method, no ambiguities can arise. There is just one complication. Assume that a method call $e.f(\ldots)$ should be compiled, where the statically known type of the expression e is an interface I. In general, it cannot be guaranteed that the method f has the same relative address in all classes A' that implement the interface I. One solution is to provide for each class A a *hash* table h_A that assigns to each *name* f of a method the code address of the corresponding implementation in A. In order to allow for an efficient implementation of such hash tables, JAVA provides the *String Pool* where all statically known strings, in particular all method names, are stored. Instead of the textual representation of the names, the references to the representatives in the String Pool can, therefore, be used as keys.

An alternative implementation, more in line with the philosophy of C++, would accommodate in an A-Object for each of the implemented interfaces I_j, a reference to a suitable method table t_{A,I_j} for I_j within the class A . The table t_{A,I_j} contains the references to the implementations of the methods declared in I_j. Each method f of the interface I_j receives a fixed relative address with which the actual start address of an implementation of f can be looked up in all tables t_{A',I_j} for implementing classes A'.

Let us assume that an expression e has the static type $I *$ for an interface I and evaluates at run-time to a pointer to an object o of a class A that implements I. The method f of a call $e \rightarrow f$ then must be looked up in the corresponding table $t_{A,I}$ of the object o. To find this table quickly, we let the pointer to the object o not point to the start of the memory block of o, but to the reference to the table $t_{A,I}$ (Fig. 5.5). This pointer represents the *I-view* to the object o. This idea incurs two problems.

- The methods declared in an interface may want to access the attributes of the object. Therefore, the table for each interface I must also contain the *distance* between the beginning of the object and the reference to the table $t_{A,I}$. This allows us to pass the *recovered* object reference to each call of a method f.

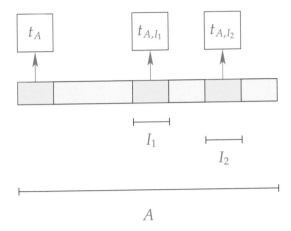

Fig. 5.5. Object of a class that implements the interfaces I_1, I_2

- On the other hand, type casts applied to references to objects may change the view and, thus, also the reference itself. When translating the assignment

$$I * x \leftarrow \textbf{new } A();$$

the I-View for the new A object must be selected by moving the pointer to the object within the object to the I-view. Only this reference is stored in the variable x.

This second kind of implementation of interfaces bypasses the use of hash tables, but has the disadvantage that the start address of a method f might have to be stored multiple times: one time in the table for A and furthermore in each table for an interface implemented by A that contains f. A generalization of the approach that we have just outlined to other forms of multiple inheritance is discussed in Exercises 4 and 5.

5.9 Exercises

The following extract of a C++ class library of graphics objects is used as a running example for the exercises in this section.

```
class graphical_object {
    virtual void translate(double x_offset, double y_offset);
    virtual void scale(double factor);
    // possibly further general methods of the class
};
class point : public graphical_object {
    double      xc, yc;
```

```
public:
  void translate(double x_offset, double y_offset) {
    xc+=                x_offset;
    yc+=                y_offset;
  }
  void scale(double factor) {
    xc*=                factor;
    yc*=                factor;
  }
  point(double x0, double y0) { xc= x0; yc= y0; }
  void set(double x0, double y0) { xc= x0; yc= y0; }
  double x(void) { return xc; }
  double y(void) { return yc; }
  double dist(point &);
};
class closed_graphical: public graphical_object {
 public:
  // area enclosed by the object
    virtual double area(void);
};
class ellipse: public closed_graphical {
  point _center;        // center of the ellipse
  double _x_radius, _y_radius;
                        // radius of the ellipse
  double _angle;        // angle from x-axis
 public:
  // Constructor
    ellipse(point &center,
            double x_radius, double y_radius,
            double angle) {
      _center= center;
      _x_radius= x_radius;   _y_radius= y_radius;
      _angel= angle;
    }
  // ellipse area -- overloads 'closed_graphical::area'
    double area(void) { return PI * _x_radius * _y_radius; }
  // distance to a point -- complex!
    virtual double dist(point &);
  // Center
    point* center(void) { return &_center; }
  // move -- overloads 'graphical_object::translate'
    void translate(double x_offset, double y_offset) {
      _center.translate(x_offset, double y_offset);
    }
  // scaling -- overloads 'graphical_object::scale'
```

```
    void scale(double scale_factor) {
      _x_radius *=    scale_factor;
      _y_radius *=    scale_factor;
    }
  // ....
};
class circle: public ellipse {
 public:
  // constructor
    circle(point &center, double radius){
      ellipse(center,radius,radius);
    }
  // distance to a point -- overloads 'ellipse::dist'
    virtual double dist(point &p) {
      double center_dist= _center.dist(p);
      if (center_dist <= radius) return 0;
      else return center_dist - radius;
    }
  // ....
};
```

1. *Methods.*   Compile the method **ellipse** :: *translate.*
2. *Virtual Method Tables.*   Determine for all classes, the relative addresses of virtual methods within the respective virtual method table. Translate a method call of the form $c.dist(p)$ where c is a circle and p is a point.
3. *Subtypes.*   The new definition of a class should not affect the existing class structure. Based on the subtyping rule, methods of already existing classes must also be able to work with objects of the new class. Through overloading of methods of parent classes, their view onto new objects can become inconsistent. Thus, redefinitions should be handled with caution. Three different aspects must be considered.
   - *The meaning (semantics) of members:*
     each attribute and each method has a meaning which should not be affected by overloading. Thus, for instance, the method *scale* is meant to scale a graphics object. A redefinition should implement the same function, both at the current level of abstraction as well as at the level of the parent class.
   - *Restrictions through the type system:*
     Redefinitions should not lead to type inconsistencies.
   - *Restrictions of the compilation schemes:*
     Redefinitions can invalidate the assumptions made at compile-time and, then, should not be permitted.

   Although the first aspect is essential, a compiler normally does not have the required specifications for verifying semantical properties. In this exercise, we consider restrictions imposed by the type system.

Casting a type into a subtype is called *type tightening*, casting a type into a supertype is called *type loosening*. A prototype (of a method) is tightened if the types of the return value are tightened and the types of the input parameters are loosened.

a) Argue that from the point of view of the type system, tightening of the prototype of a redefined method can be allowed.

Show through examples that the prototypes of virtual methods can at most be tightened; any other modification may lead to type errors at calls that were previously correct.

Argue that a non-tightened modification of the prototype for a redefined *private* method is also only acceptable under restricted assumptions. For a modification to be admissable, properties of the parent class are required, beyond the types of its attributes and the prototypes of its methods – which properties?

b) The language EIFFEL allows a derived class to tighten the type of an inherited attribute. Explain why attributes can then only be *read* by a foreign class.

Show through an example that tightening the type of an attribute is only allowed under restricted assumptions. For a modification to be admissable, properties of the parent class are required, beyond the types of its attributes and the prototypes of its methods – which properties?

4. *Multiple inheritance I.*   In this exercise we consider multiple inheritance. For simplicity, we assume that from each parent class B exactly one instance is inherited by a subclass A, which means that each A-object contains exactly one B-subobject.

For each parent class B of A, a fixed memory block is allocated within the memory block of an object of the class A. Also, we assume that the first immediate parent class B_1 is treated like the immediate parent class in the case of single inheritance: its memory block is located at the beginning of the memory block for the immediate subclass A (Fig. 5.6).

For a parent class B_i, the B_i-*view* to an object of class A is obtained by placing a pointer at the start of the block designated for B_i. Accordingly, the A-view to the object agrees with the B_1-view for the first immediate parent class B_1 of A. Within the memory block for A, a reference to the table t_A of all virtual functions known in A is stored in location 0. At the beginning of all parent classes B_i which are not the first immediate parent class, a reference to a table t_{A,B_i} is stored. The table t_{A,B_i} contains the start addresses of all methods of A that are known in B_i. This construction is recursively applied to all parent classes of immediate parent classes B_i of A, and so on.

A method f known in B_i may have been overloaded by the subclass A. Thus in t_{A,B_i}, not only the start address of f must be recorded, but also the *distance* between the memory blocks for the classes A and B_i. This allows us to construct before the call to f, from B_i the correct A-view to the A-object.

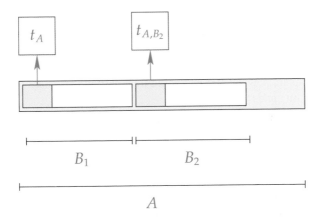

Fig. 5.6. The object organization for two parent classes

a) Complete the details of the definitions of the tables t_{A,B_i}. Implement the type cast of a pointer to an A-object to a pointer to an object of a super- and a subclass of A, respectively.

b) Discuss strategies for resolving name conflicts and sketch their implementations.

c) Combine the basic principle for multiple inheritance with our former translation schemes.

d) Test your new translation schemes on our example class library.

5. *Multiple inheritance II.*   In this exercise, we again consider multiple inheritance. As in Exercise 4 we assume that each parent class B is inherited by the subclass A only once. For each non-first parent class B, the object organization in Exercise 4 stores a dedicated table $t_{A,B}$ for the virtual methods of class A that are visible in B. Thus, all methods from $t_{A,B}$ are also contained in t_A. We want to eliminate this inefficiency.

Our goal is to save a virtual method known to B only in the table $t_{A,B}$ and not in the tables t_A and $t_{A',B}$ for classes A' between A and B. For this, the address environment for class A is modified such that $\rho_A(f)$ returns a pair $\langle d_t, i \rangle$ where d_t is the relative address of the reference to the table t, and i is the index where the start address for f in t is recorded. Following the start address $\_f$, the table t memorizes the relative distance d_t for recovering the A-view of the object. Relative to an A-view a to an object, we obtain the start address of the pair $(\_f, d_t)$ for the method f by:

$$S[a + d_t] + 2 \cdot i$$

(a) Modify the call to a virtual method according to this optimization.

(b) Estimate the savings that this optimization offers.

(c) Give an algorithm that computes, for a given class hierarchy, the distances $d_{A,B}$, the address environment ρ_A for virtual functions of A, and constructs the required tables.

6. *Generics.*   Implement a generic class for queues, that is first-in-first-out queues. Explain how a compiler should treat multiple instances of queues, such as queue$\langle$**int**$\rangle$ and queue$\langle$list$\rangle$.

5.10 List of Additional Registers

COP, Current Object Pointer   p. 162

5.11 CMa Instructions for Objects

loadm	p. 163	**loadsc**	p. 164
loadmc	p. 163	**loadv**	p. 164
loads	p. 164	**storem**	p. 163

5.12 References

SIMULA67, the predecessor of object-oriented languages is described in [DN66] and [Sim87]. The standard reference for SMALLTALK is [GR83]; SMALLTALK and the associated virtual machine VISUALWORKS can be found in [GH98]. C++ is defined in [Str00]. The basis for the standardization of C++ by ANSI is [ES90]. [Mey88] and [Mey92] provide an introduction to EIFFEL. [Cox86] describes OBJECTIVE-C. Object-oriented extensions to LISP are described in [BS82, Can80]. An interesting modern object-oriented programming language is Scala [OAC+04].

There are numerous books on JAVA and C#. An overview of the implementation of object-oriented programming languages such as SMALLTALK, JAVA and C++ is given in [BH98]. The technical basis of common virtual machines for JAVA is explained in the JAVA Virtual Machine specification [LY99]. Krall presents techniques for Just-In-Time compilation [Kra98]. Stärk et al. [SSB01] offer a formalization of the JVM and discuss correctness issues.

Some further approaches to the implementation of JAVA or C# is offered by the .NET framework with the Common Language Runtime (CLR) [ECM06, MG00]. The works in [Gou01, Sin03] provide a comparison of these two approaches.

References

[ACKM03] Gustavo Alonso, Fabio Casati, Harumi Kuno, Vijay Machiraju. *Web Services.* Springer, 2003.

[AK91] H. Aït-Kaci. *Warren's Abstract Machine: A Tutorial Reconstruction.* MIT Press, 1991.

[Amm81] U. Ammann. *Code Generation of a Pascal-Compiler.* In [Bar81], 1981.

[Apt90] K.R. Apt. *Logic Programming, Handbook of Theoretical Computer Science.* Elsevier, 1990.

[AW06] Krzysztof Apt, Mark Wallace. *Constraint Logic Programming Using ECLiPSe.* Cambridge University Press, 2006.

[Bar81] D.W. Barron (Hrsg.). *Pascal: The Language and Its Implementation.* Wiley, 1981.

[Bez88] M. Bezem. *Logic Programming and PROLOG.* In CWI Quarterly **1**(3), pp. 15–29, Amsterdam, Centre for Mathematics and Computer Science, 1988.

[BH98] Bernhard Bauer, Riitta Höllerer. *Übersetzung objektorientierter Programmiersprachen: Konzepte, abstrakte Maschinen und Praktikum.* Springer, 1998.

[Bru04] Michael Brundage. *XQuery: The XML Query Language.* Addison-Wesley, 2004.

[BS82] Daniel G. Bobrow, Mark J. Stefik. *LOOPS: An Object-Oriented Programming System for Interlisp*, 1982.

[Can80] H. I. Cannon. Flavors. Technical Report, MIT Artificial Intelligence Laboratory, 1980.

[CM03] W.F. Clocksin, C.S. Mellish. *Programming in Prolog: Using the ISO Standard.* Springer, 2003.

[Cox86] Brad J. Cox. *Object-Oriented Programming: An Evolutionary Approach.* Addison-Wesley, 1986.

[DN66] Ole-Johan Dahl, Kristen Nygaard. Simula: An Algol-Based Simulation Language. *Communications of the ACM (CACM)*, 9(9):671–678, 1966.

[ECM06] Common Language Infrastructure (CLI). 4th ed.. Technical Report ECMA-335, ECMA International, 2006.

[ES90] Margaret A. Ellis, Bjarne Stroustrup. *The Annotated C++ Reference Manual.* Addison-Wesley, 1990.

[FW87] J. Fairbairn, S.C. Wray. *TIM. A Simple, Lazy Abstract Machine to Execute Supercombinators.* In Proc. Functional Programming Languages and Computer Architecture, LNCS 274, pp. 34–45. Springer, 1987.

R. Wilhelm, H. Seidl, *Compiler Design*, DOI 10.1007/978-3-642-14909-2,

[GH98]   Adele Goldberg, Timothy Howard. *The Smalltalk Developer's Guide to Visual-Works with Disk*. Advances in Object Technology. Cambridge University Press, 1998.

[Gou01]   K. John Gough. *Stacking Them up: A Comparison of Virtual Machines*. In 6th Australasian Computer Systems Architecture Conference (ACSAC), pp. 55–61, 2001.

[GR83]   Adele Goldberg, David Robson. *Smalltalk-80: The Language and Its Implementation*. Addison-Wesley, 1983.

[Han86]   M. Hanus. *Problemlösen mit Prolog*. Teubner Verlag, 1986.

[Hau06]   Tobias Hauser. *Einstieg in ActionScript*. Galileo Press, 2006.

[HS99]   Michael Hanus, Ramin Sadre. An Abstract Machine for Curry and Its Concurrent Implementation in Java. *Journal of Functional and Logic Programming*, Special Issue 1, 1999.

[Inc99]   Adobe Systems Inc. *PostScript(R) Language Reference (3rd ed.)*. Addison-Wesley, 1999.

[JL96]   Richard Jones, Rafael Lins. *Garbage Collection: Algorithms for Automatic Dynamic Memory Management*. Wiley, New York, 1996.

[Joh84]   T. Johnsson. *Efficient Compilation of Lazy Evaluation*. In Proc. ACM SIGPLAN 84 Symposium on Compiler Construction, SIGPLAN Notices **19**(6), pp. 58–69, 1984.

[Jon92]   Simon L. Peyton Jones. Implementing lazy functional languages on stock hardware: the Spineless Tagless G-machine. *Journal of Functional Programming (JFP)*, 2(2):127–202, 1992.

[Kay04]   Michael Kay. *XSLT 2.0 Programmer's Reference (3rd ed.)*. Wrox, 2004.

[KBS86]   H. Kleine-Büning, S. Schmittgen. *Prolog*. Teubner, 1986.

[KCD⁺03]   Howard Katz, Don Chamberlin, Denise Draper, Mary Fernandez, Michael Kay, Jonathan Robie, Michael Rys, Jerome Simeon, Jim Tivy, Philip Wadler. *XQuery from the Experts: A Guide to the W3C XML Query Language*. Addison-Wesley, 2003.

[Kra98]   Andreas Krall. *Efficient JavaVM Just-in-Time Compilation*. In IEEE International Conference on Parallel Architectures and Compilation Techniques (PACT), pp. 205–212, 1998.

[Lan64]   P.J. Landin. *The Mechanical Evaluation of Expressions*. In Computer Journal **6**(4), 1964.

[Ler90]   Xavier Leroy. The ZINC Experiment: An Economical Implementation of the ML Language. Technical Report RT-0117, INRIA, Rocquencourt, February 1990.

[Llo87]   J.W. Lloyd. *Foundations of Logic Programming*. 2nd ed., Springer, 1987.

[LY99]   Tim Lindholm, Frank Yellin. *Java Virtual Maschine Specification. 2nd ed.*. SUN Microsystems Inc., 1999.

[Mey88]   Bertrand Meyer. *Object-Oriented Software Construction*. Prentice Hall, 1988.

[Mey92]   Bertrand Meyer. *Eiffel. The Language*. Prentice-Hall, 1992.

[MG00]   Eric Meijer, Jeremy Gough. Technical Overview of the Common Language Runtime, 2000.

[MW88]   D. Maier, D.S. Warren. *Computing with Logic, Logic Programming with Prolog*. Benjamin/Cummings, 1988.

[OAC⁺04]   Martin Odersky, Philippe Altherr, Vincent Cremet, Burak Emir, Sebastian Maneth, Stéphane Micheloud, Nikolay Mihaylov, Michel Schinz, Erik Stenman, Matthias Zenger. An Overview of the Scala Programming Language. Technical report, EPFL-LAMP, 2004.

[PD82]   St. Pemberton, M. Daniels. *Pascal Implementation, The P4 Compiler.* Ellis Horwood, 1982.

[Ped04]   Volnei A. Pedroni. *Circuit Design with VHDL.* MIT Press, 2004.

[PJ87]   S.L. Peyton Jones. *The Implementation of Functional Programming Languages.* Prentice Hall, 1987.

[RR64]   B. Randell, L.J. Russell. *Algol60 Implementation.* Academic Press, 1964.

[Sco05]   Michael L. Scott. *Programming Language Pragmatics (2nd ed.).* Morgan Kaufmann, 2005.

[Seb05]   Robert W. Sebesta. *Concepts of Programming Languages (7th ed.).* Addison-Wesley, 2005.

[SIC06]   SICStus   4   Beta   Documentation,   2006.   Homepage: `http://www.sics.se/isl/sicstuswww/site/`.

[Sim87]   *SIS, Data Processing Programming Languages: SIMULA*, 1987. Svensk Standard SS 636114.

[Sin03]   Jeremy Singer. JVM Versus CLR: A Comparative Study. *Proceedings of the 2nd Int. Conf. on Principles and Practice of Programming in Java*, pp. 167–169, 2003.

[SN05]   Jim Smith, Ravi Nair. *Virtual Machines: Versatile Platforms for Systems and Processes.* The Morgan Kaufmann Series in Computer Architecture and Design. Morgan Kaufmann, 2005.

[SS94]   L. Sterling, E. Shapiro. *The Art of Prolog, Advanced Programming Techniques.* MIT Press, 1994.

[SSB01]   Roland Stärk, Joachim Schmid, Egon Börger. *Java and the Virtual Machine Definition, Verification, Validation.* Springer, 2001.

[Str00]   Bjarne Stroustrup. *The C++ Programming Language. Special Edition.* Addison-Wesley, 2000.

[SWD05]   Tom Schrijvers, Jan Wielemaker, Bart Demoen. *Constraint Handling Rules for SWI-Prolog.* In Workshop on (Constraint) Logic Programming, Ulm, 2005.

[TN06]   Allen B Tucker, Robert Noonan. *Programming Languages.* McGraw-Hill Science, 2006.

[VSD02]   Ruben Vandeginste, Konstantinos F. Sagonas, Bart Demoen. *Segment Order Preserving and Generational Garbage Collection for Prolog.* In Practical Aspects of Declarative Languages, 4th Int. Symposium (PADL), pp. 299–317. Springer, LNCS 2257, 2002.

[War77]   D.H.D. Warren. *Applied Logic: Its Use and Implementation as a Programming Language Tool.* Ph.D. Thesis, Univ. of Edinburgh, 1977.

[War83]   D.H.D. Warren. *An Abstract PROLOG Instruction Set.* Technical Note 309, SRI International, 1983.

[Wil92]   Paul R. Wilson. *Uniprocessor Garbage Collection Techniques.* In Proc. Int. Workshop on Memory Management (IWMM), pp. 1–42. Springer, LNCS 637, 1992.

[WNST06]   Daniel Wasserrab, Tobias Nipkow, Gregor Snelting, Frank Tip. *An Operational Semantics and Type Safety Proof for Multiple Inheritance in C++.* In 21st Annu. ACM SIGPLAN Conf. on Object-Oriented Programming, Systems, Languages, and Applications (OOPSLA), pp. 345–362, 2006.

Index

Printing: Ten Brink, Meppel, The Netherlands
Binding: Stürtz, Würzburg, Germany